Land

Resources

Peter Dauvergne & Jane Lister, *Timber*
Michael Nest, *Coltan*
Elizabeth R. DeSombre & J. Samuel Barkin, *Fish*
Jennifer Clapp, *Food*
David Feldman, *Water*
Gavin Bridge & Philippe Le Billon, *Oil*

Land

DEREK HALL

polity

The right of Derek Hall to be identified as Author of this Work has been
asserted in accordance with the UK Copyright, Designs and Patents Act 1988.

First published in 2013 by Polity Press

Polity Press
65 Bridge Street
Cambridge CB2 1UR, UK

Polity Press
350 Main Street
Malden, MA 02148, USA

ISBN-13: 978-0-7456-5277-1(pb)
ISBN-13: 978-0-7456-5276-4

A catalogue record for this book is available from the British Library.

Typeset in 10.25 on 13 pt Scala
by Servis Filmsetting Ltd, Stockport, Cheshire
Printed and bound in Great Britain by the MPG Books Group

The publisher has used its best endeavours to ensure that the URLs for
external websites referred to in this book are correct and active at the time of
going to press. However, the publisher has no responsibility for the websites
and can make no guarantee that a site will remain live or that the content is or
will remain appropriate.

Every effort has been made to trace all copyright holders, but if any have been
inadvertently overlooked the publisher will be pleased to include any necessary
credits in any subsequent reprint or edition.

For further information on Polity, visit our website: www.politybooks.com

Contents

Figures and Tables

Acronyms

BCN	Biodiversity Conservation Network
BIA	Bangalore International Airport
BINGO	big international non-governmental organization
BMIC	Bangalore-Mysore Infrastructure Corridor
BSP	Biodiversity Support Program
CBNRM	community-based natural resource management
CFS	Committee on World Food Security
CIA	Central Intelligence Agency
CITES	Convention on International Trade in Endangered Species of Wild Fauna and Flora
CMWMA	Crater Mountain Wildlife Management Area
COW	Correlates of War
EEA	European Economic Area
EEZ	Exclusive Economic Zone
FAO	Food and Agriculture Organization of the United Nations
FATA	Federally Administered Tribal Areas
FCR	Frontier Crimes Regulations
FDI	foreign direct investment
FIAN	Food First International Action Network
GDP	Gross Domestic Product
GPS	Global Positioning System
ICDP	integrated conservation and development project
ICJ	International Court of Justice
IFAD	International Fund for Agricultural Development
IFI	international financial institution

ILD	Institute for Liberty and Democracy
ILO	International Labour Organization
IMF	International Monetary Fund
ISI	Directorate for Inter-Service Intelligence
IT	information technology
IUCN	International Union for Conservation of Nature
KIADB	Karnataka Industrial Areas Development Board
LRAN	Land Research Action Network
MCA	Millennium Challenge Account
MLAR	market-led agrarian reform
MWC	Mahindra World City
NATO	North Atlantic Treaty Organization
NGO	non-governmental organization
NWFP	North-West Frontier Province
OED	Oxford English Dictionary
PA	political agent
PNG	Papua New Guinea
PRC	People's Republic of China
RAI	Principles for Responsible Agricultural Investment
RCF	Research and Conservation Foundation of Papua New Guinea
ROC	Republic of China
SEZ	Special Economic Zone
TNC	transnational corporation
UN	United Nations
UNCLOS	UN Convention on the Law of the Sea
UNCTAD	UN Conference on Trade and Development
UNDRIP	UN Declaration on the Rights of Indigenous Peoples
UNEP	UN Environment Programme
UNESCO	UN Educational, Scientific and Cultural Organization

USAID	United States Agency for International Development
WCMC	World Conservation Monitoring Centre
WCS	Wildlife Conservation Society
WDPA	World Database on Protected Areas
WWF	World Wide Fund for Nature

Acknowledgements

My thinking about land has been deeply shaped by two highly enjoyable experiences. One was my participation in ChATSEA (Challenges of the Agrarian Transition in Southeast Asia), a research project funded by Canada's Social Sciences and Humanities Research Council and coordinated by Rodolphe De Koninck. It was through ChATSEA that I had the opportunity to co-author *Powers of Exclusion: Land Dilemmas in Southeast Asia* with Philip Hirsch and Tania Murray Li, and this book has been strongly influenced by what I learned about land from them. The other was the year I spent as an S. V. Ciriacy-Wantrup Visiting Research Fellow in the Department of Environmental Science, Policy and Management at the University of California, Berkeley. My participation in 'Land Lab' and my conversations with, especially, Mike Dwyer, Louise Fortmann, Alice Kelly, Christian Lund, Nancy Peluso, Noer Fauzi Rachman, Kevin Woods and Megan Ybarra helped me greatly in the initial formulation of the framework of this book.

The first draft of this manuscript was the subject of a January 2012 book workshop that was generously funded by the Balsillie School of International Affairs. I would like to thank Lauren Judge for her organizational work on the workshop, and the participants whose detailed and thoughtful feedback made this a much better book: Haroon Akram-Lodhi, Kim Burnett, Taarini Chopra, Jennifer Clapp, Will Coleman, Michael Eilenberg, Ariane Goetz, Eric Helleiner, Tania

Murray Li, Sarah Martin, Marie-Josée Massicotte and Yasmine Shamsie. I also received invaluable comments and advice from Jennifer Beck, June Hall, Elizabeth Havice, Michael Levien, Dann Naseemullah, Matthew Rudolph, Vasundhara Sirnate, John Wadland, Wendy Wolford and an anonymous reviewer, and Gail Ferguson did a wonderful job of copy editing. Louise Knight and David Winters at Polity were terrifically supportive and did an enormous amount to make the writing and publishing process as smooth as possible. Lisa Stadelmeyer provided excellent research assistance in the early stages of the project. I am extremely grateful for all of this help, but I alone am responsible for any errors in the final product. Anne-Marie Colpron and Alicia Sliwinski gave me the bottle of whisky mentioned in chapter 7.

Finally, I would like to thank Tanya Richardson for her encouragement, her comments on and suggestions for the manuscript and for taking care of our own plot of land while my head was stuck in this book.

CHAPTER ONE

Introduction

Huang's saga

In August 2011, Chinese businessman Huang Nubo announced that his company, Zhongkun Group, intended to buy a large tract of land in north-eastern Iceland.[1] Huang's intention was to invest more than US$100 million (including US$9 million for the land) to build an ecotourism resort that would feature among its attractions a luxury hotel, a golf course, a race track and hot-air balloon rides. Huang, who was described in media coverage as an adventurer and a poet, hoped that the resort would appeal to tourists from China and India keen to get away from their crowded city lives and experience solitude and wilderness. The site, in Grímsstaðir, offered plenty of both: 300 km² of land (about 0.3 per cent of Iceland's territory) in a bleak and sparsely populated region just south of the Arctic Circle. To buy the land, however, Huang needed to do more than hand over the money. The deal required government approval not only because the proposed area included both private and state-owned land but because of a law restricting land sales to investors from outside the European Economic Area (EEA) from buying large amounts of land in Iceland. Huang duly applied for an exemption to this law.

Huang's proposal split Icelandic opinion, and the ensuing debate raised profound questions about the place of land in Iceland's national life and international relations. Proponents pointed out that Iceland was in desperate need of foreign investment as it struggled to recover from the devastating financial and currency crisis that had struck the country in 2008. Some felt that China would be an excellent source of such investment. Iceland's president, Ólafur Ragnar Grímsson, stated pointedly that after the crisis 'China and India lent Iceland a helping hand in many constructive ways, whereas Europe was hostile and the US was absent.' Critics of the deal, on the other hand, raised concerns about selling such a large tract of national land to a foreigner. They also pointed to Huang's past as a government official (in China's Ministry of Construction and in the propaganda department of the Communist Party of China Central Committee) to argue that his bid should not be taken at face value as a private business proposition. Rather, they suspected that the geopolitical ambitions of the Chinese government lay behind the deal. With both land and sea ice receding in the Arctic, the region is seeing rapid growth in resource exploration and extraction, and the Arctic Ocean may soon become viable as a shipping route between Europe and East Asia. Icelandic officials have in fact been promoting their country as a logistics hub for Arctic resource exploration and shipping, and Chinese diplomatic activity related to the Arctic has been increasing. Critics thus saw in the proposed deal not an innocent ecotourism resort but a toehold for the Chinese government. Proponents countered that these claims were hard to square with the fact that the project would include no land with access to the coast. Huang, for his part, called the accusations absurd and emphasized the purely private nature of the deal – though he may have undermined his case by playing with his cat during a video interview, a move uncomfortably reminiscent of the James Bond villain Ernst Stavro Blofeld (not to mention Dr Evil in the *Austin Powers* movies).

The deal did not go through. In late November 2011, Iceland's Minister of the Interior Ögmundur Jónasson announced that Huang's application for an exemption from the law had been turned down. The ministry listed a number of criteria that non-EEA companies looking to buy land had to meet and found that the Zhongkun Group did not meet any of them. It also argued that the sheer amount of land involved meant that an exemption would set a dangerous precedent. Jónasson worried, too, about the 'fire sale' characteristics of the deal, stating that 'When a nation is in distress and its currency is weak, that is the time to be on your guard against those who would attempt to buy our national resources cheaply.' While the decision was the interior minister's to make, the two governing parties had by now taken quite different stances on it, with the Left Greens (Jónasson's party) opposed and the Social Democrats more in favour. The prime minister and the foreign and economic ministries joined President Grímsson in supporting the investment, and one Social Democrat MP described the rejection as 'crazy', 'deplorable' and 'devastating'. A former finance minister argued in favour of the deal by invoking the reputation that Icelandic businessmen had acquired since the financial crisis, asking 'Who would you prefer to own a large Icelandic farm: a poetry-writing, nature-loving Chinese businessman, or one of our homegrown criminal Viking raiders?' The poet, meanwhile, lashed out at the rejection, claiming that he had not been made aware of the criteria cited by the Interior Ministry in turning down his application. He also made the broader point that this was far from the only example in recent years of western rejection of Chinese investment. Huang complained that 'The Western world asks us to open the Chinese market without restrictions, but when it's a question of their resources they close the door on us.' Other commentators, however, rushed to point out that China forbids land sales not only to foreigners, but to its own citizens.

Combining as it does the ongoing fallout from the 2008

financial crisis, the rising economic power of China and western responses to it, and the politics of Arctic resource development and shipping in a warming world, Huang's saga[2] dramatically illustrates the changes taking place in the global political economy in the early twenty-first century. The story also calls attention to the complex and multifaceted role that land plays in relations between countries. It highlights, for instance, a common debate over the purchase of land by foreigners. In Iceland as elsewhere, one side of this debate emphasizes the economic benefits that such investments are meant to bring (including job creation and contributions to government revenues), while the other focuses on the threats – economic, political and otherwise – they may pose. Starkly put, one side sees an idle resource that someone wants to put to productive use, while the other sees the alienation of part of the national territory. Such debates are not carried out in a legal vacuum: Iceland, like most countries, has laws and regulations governing the acquisition of land by foreigners.

The Grímsstaðir case also shows that concerns over land acquisition can be given extra impetus by the nationality of the would-be purchaser. This is far from the only large piece of land in a foreign country that Chinese investors have tried to purchase or lease in recent years. Arguments over Huang's resort took place in the shadow of widespread concerns about a global 'land grab' in which transnational corporations and states are moving to take control over vast areas of land in foreign countries. The fact that some of these investments are being orchestrated by state agencies from non-democratic countries like China has deepened the nervousness that usually attends foreign purchases and long-term leases of land. Control over land, indeed, is wrapped up with anxiety over national security and geopolitics. In the Icelandic case, the worry is over China's alleged drive to project power in the Arctic; elsewhere, the key issue may be the ability of countries to grow enough food to feed themselves, or the acquisition by foreigners of land in sensitive border areas.

Land and the human relationship with it are enormous topics, far too big to cover in a short (or even a long) book. I argue, however, that we can gain particularly valuable insights into contemporary dynamics around land by focusing on the transnational relationships associated with it. I define these as the efforts made by various actors to exert control over land across international borders, together with the cross-border politics and relationships (including corporate connections, activist networks and flows of ideas) that help to shape control over land. I argue as well that, in order to understand these dynamics, we need to recognize that they concern three different and very fundamental things. These are the relationships between land, authority and identity that create *territory*; *regulation*, or the governance of how land is held and used; and the control of specific pieces of land as *property*.[3]

Transnational dynamics around territory, regulation and property are far from new. In each of these areas, however, there are major changes afoot that this book seeks to explain. With respect to *territory*, the most important contemporary issues relate to the efforts of states to exert control of land both across borders and within their own, and the responses by other states and by non-state groups to those efforts. The aspects of these struggles that most demand our attention are the near-disappearance, since the late 1970s, of the redistribution of territory through interstate war; the complex politics of control over the extensive 'frontier' areas that exist within many states; and the rise of transnational movements pressing for recognition of indigenous rights to land. In the sphere of *regulation*, there has been an enormous increase in attempts by transnational actors to influence the rules that govern land use, especially in the South. Such attempts have been spearheaded by a remarkably wide range of groups, including states, international financial institutions (IFIs), transnational corporations (TNCs), non-governmental organizations (NGOs), organizations of the United Nations (UN), private foundations, and environmental certification organizations. These groups have sought to transform regulations regarding how property is held, the rights of indigenous peoples and environmental conservation. With respect to *property*, finally, the most high-profile recent changes have involved TNCs and states seeking to buy or lease land in other countries, and activists organizing transnationally to resist this 'global land grab'. Transnational relations have also been central to the widespread expansion of conservation areas and of special economic zones in the South, both of which have seen changes in the property status of large amounts of land.

This introductory chapter lays the groundwork for the analysis of the transnational dynamics of territory, regulation and property in the chapters to come. In the next section, I ask what land is, and discuss some of the aspects of land that differentiate it from other resources and complicate efforts to understand it in a unified way (while also making the project an especially interesting one). The subsequent section explains the concepts of territory, regulation and property that underpin the book's analysis. I then provide brief introductions to the main themes of the book's topical chapters, themes which add up to an overview of the key issues involved in transnational struggles over land control today. The last section highlights other issues related to land control that the book does not address.

What is land, and how is it different from other resources?

Asking 'what is land?' may seem like an odd, and unnecessary, place to start. What could be more concrete and obvious than the ground beneath our feet? The *Oxford English Dictionary*'s definition of 'land' as 'The solid portion of the earth's surface, as opposed to *sea, water*'[4] seems straightforward enough. But things are not so simple. There is, first, something peculiarly abstract about 'land' when you stop to think about it. If you were to remove all the vegetation and soil from a hectare of land, you would still have a hectare of land (though rather less productive and of rather lower elevation). If you continued on into the rock and minerals below and started removing them in turn, it is not clear how deep you would have to dig before there would no longer be 'land' there. Indeed, the *OED* definition means you cannot get rid of land in this way; for a given area to stop being land, you have to drown it. This abstract quality makes it difficult to visualize 'land' as such, as opposed to the soil and rocks that constitute land and the vegetation that sits on top of it, all of which can be carted away without diminishing land's landness. Second, the *OED*'s seemingly clear definition of land as 'not-water' hides a good deal of ambiguity. Plenty of areas straddle the boundary between the solid and the liquid. River deltas, floodplains, tidal zones, seasonal ponds, marshes and swamps all combine land and water. New technology (like underwater drilling) and new legal frameworks (like the UN Convention on the Law of the Sea) have also increasingly led to parts of the seabed – unambiguously under water, all the time – being treated in many respects as land. The question of whether such areas should be considered 'land' – and, if so, when – is not settled by the objective physical definition in the *OED* but by human laws and regulations that determine how these areas can be used and held.

This book is part of a series on resources. Land, however, differs from other resources in fundamental respects. An overview of some of the key differences provides context for the approach to analysing land control outlined in the next section. The first difference is a very simple one that follows from the discussion in the previous paragraph: land does not move. Land is fixed in place and cannot be exported, or even relocated to the next town or down the road (even if, again, the soil and minerals that constitute land can be so moved). If you want to use land, it will not come to you – you have to go to it, or convince other people to go to it for you. For this reason, this book cannot take the common approach to studying resources of investigating the 'commodity chain' connecting the point of production or extraction with the point of consumption. We cannot follow land, as we can corn, coltan, coffee and cocaine, as it changes hands and is transformed on its journey to the final consumer. Partly for this reason, too, the phenomenon in which control of a resource is intensely concentrated at some point in the commodity chain does not apply to land. Fifteen companies control four-fifths of the world's proven oil reserves, and 75–90 per cent of world trade in grains and oilseeds, like corn, soy and wheat, is in the hands of just four firms.[5] While the control of land – in all the different senses of that term to be discussed in the next section – is highly unequal, it is not as unequal as this. No private company owns more than a minuscule portion of the earth's surface, and even the territory of Russia, the biggest country by area, covers only around 11 per cent of the world's roughly 149 million km² of land.

Land, second, is extremely heterogeneous. Many resources are seen to have a world market price that, while certainly a simplification (one common measure of the 'price of oil', for instance, actually refers to the price of West Texas Intermediate light sweet crude), is still a meaningful indicator that conveys information about what you could expect to pay for a barrel of oil, a bushel of wheat or an ounce of gold. The price of land is more like the price of labour. Land and labour both vary so dramatically in location and quality that the notion of a benchmark world price for a generic day's work or hectare of land is nonsensical. One thousand hectares of land can be had in plenty of places for literally nothing (or less), while a few square metres in some downtown business districts can cost as much as – well, if you have to ask, you wouldn't be able to afford it. There is no reason to expect that a spike or collapse in the price of land in one part of the world will be accompanied by similar movements elsewhere. Land price variations can verge on the bizarre. It has been estimated that if the people of Japan had sold all of their country's land at the peak of a land-price bubble in the late 1980s, they would have been able to buy all the land in the rest of the world with the proceeds.

A third difference is that control over land is indispensable to almost all human activity. Some form of control over land is often (though by no means always) necessary for access to both non-renewable resources, like uranium, iron ore and coltan, and to renewable ones, like water, trees and soil. In terrestrial environments, land control is also wrapped up with control over ecosystems. Conservationists wishing to preserve biodiversity generally need to exercise some kind of control over land to do so. Land can also be a sink – a place to dump stuff that you no longer want. Finally and most basically, land provides space for human action, whether it be used for agriculture, housing, industry, infrastructure, tourism or what have you. Land, in short, is different because efforts to control it are woven together with almost everything that people do.

A fourth difference, and one that harks back again to the abstract nature of land, is that land is commonly rented. This is not true of other resources. It is difficult to think of circumstances (other than the staging of an avant-garde play) under which someone might want to borrow 12 tons of iron ore or 500 kilograms of fish. The reason holders of a piece of land are often willing to lend it to someone else is that land as such is not consumed through use in the way that other resources are, even if overuse can degrade or ruin land for specific purposes. Land that has been stripped of its fertility by grazing or cultivation, or polluted by mining or factory effluent, or even so badly irradiated that people can no longer go anywhere near it, is still land. Indeed, people not only rent land, they do so for very long periods. In agriculture, forestry and mining, land leases of periods like 30, 50 and 99 years are the norm. The Guinness brewery in St James Gate, Dublin, has been operating since 1759 under a 9,000-year lease. We will see in the next section of this chapter that leases (like ownership) can convey some or all of a wide range of different rights to make use of the land. A forestry concession, for instance, might include the right to plant, harvest and manage timber, but not to plant cotton or to extract sub-surface resources. One lease is not at all the same as another.

Finally, land differs from other resources as a result of the power and depth of the attachments people feel to it. This is true at the level of individuals and families, who may have strong emotional connections to the family home, farm, ranch, or cottage. It is true of the ties people can feel to the neighbourhood or village in which they live or in which they grew up. More importantly for this book, it is also true at the level of larger political and ethnic groups, which almost always understand some part of the earth's surface to be their land or, in the terms I use here, their territory. Connections to and images of this land may form an important component of a group's identity. People do, of course, relate to resources other than land in emotional and identity terms. All of a country's resources, for instance, can be understood to comprise a part of the national patrimony; one has only to put the words 'hands off' in front of 'our oil', 'our fish' or 'our water' to see this. The depths of our emotional relationships to land, however, *are* unusual in this respect, and the consequences of this difference run through this book.

Territory, regulation and property

The different facets of the contemporary transnational politics of land that we encountered in Huang's saga, and some of the discussion of how land differs from other resources in the preceding section, suggest that there are a number of forms of control over land. This diversity can be organized by highlighting *territory, regulation* and *property* as the three central elements of land control over which people struggle within and across international borders. While there are enormous literatures dealing with each of these three terms and a vast range of conflicting definitions, I use them in this book to mean specific things. *Territory* refers to the relationship between land and identity, and to the existence of (or aspiration for) political authority over land. *Regulation* means the rules that govern the possession and use of land. And *property* involves the question of who has the right to decide what will be done with any particular piece of land within existing regulations.

The concept of *territory* calls attention to the ways that groups see themselves (and are seen by others) as having a deep and special connection to some reasonably specific piece of the earth's surface, an aspect of their identity that usually includes a claim to at least some political authority over 'their' land. This claim goes well beyond the regulation of land use (to be discussed below) to encompass the much wider set of powers involved in governing people, including powers over things like taxation and law. The claim can be made by many different kinds of groups – by, for instance, the residents of urban neighbourhoods or villages. In recent times, the collectivities that most commonly have been seen to have legitimate claims to authority over 'their' territory are states, nations and ethnic and indigenous groups. Other eras, however, have seen things differently: the relevant groups in medieval

Europe, for instance, would have included aristocratic line-ages that viewed their territory in patrimonial terms. The kinds of relationship that are taken to exist between identity, authority and land have also varied a great deal with time and space.

The dominant modern understanding of the relationship between territory and authority is historically unusual in several core respects. This understanding, first, locates authority over territory with states which now claim sovereign authority over virtually all of the earth's land (outside Antarctica). Most of the earlier political orders, on the other hand, were characterized by a sharing of authority between different types of bodies, including monarchs, towns, villages, aristocracies and religious orders, and did not assume that all land was subject to somebody's sovereignty. Second, the dominant understanding sees land as being under the authority of one and only one state, and assumes that states (like sub-national political units and pieces of property) will be separated from one another with surgical precision by linear borders. Third, states are taken to have exclusive authority within their own borders and no authority outside them; this distinction is often taken to mark the boundaries between domestic and international politics. All of these features of the dominant understanding add up to a very close relationship between territory, authority and the state – indeed, states are now defined in part by their borders, and a state cannot exist if it does not have any land.

The modern territory–authority relationship is also profoundly structured by our understanding of the relationship between states and nations. The nation can be defined for our purposes as a political community that is limited, sovereign and made up of members who are understood to be equal.[6] Modern states are usually conceptualized as representing and governing on behalf of nations. This tight connection between ideas of state and nation – so tight that the terms are often used interchangeably – contributes to the very strong emotional attachments citizens feel to the territory (land) of their state. The silhouette of a state's boundary is on a par with the national flag as one of the most immediately recognizable and evocative ways of graphically representing the state.[7] The modern combination of sharply defined borders, unitary sovereignty and nationalism means that once-common ways in which rulers related to territory, including receiving it through inheritance or giving it away, are now unthinkable. It also gives understandings of territory a peculiar precision: this piece of land two metres inside the country's border is our territory, to be defended to the death, while that piece two metres outside the border is no concern of ours.

Three issues complicate too-easy assumptions about the relations between linear borders, state sovereignty and nations. Care must be taken, first, with the assumption that the nation comes first and the state 'represents' it. Many of the nations we take for granted today are substantially the creation of state leaders through a process Benedict Anderson (following Hugh Seton-Watson) calls 'official nationalism'. Often, too, the 'people' – the citizens of the state – end up being a very different group to the putative nation. Second, there is a 'vertical' hierarchy of levels of government within states. This hierarchy generally includes not only the central government but also governments at the provincial/prefectural/state and at the county/municipal level. Identity and authority are distributed between these various levels of 'the state'. In countries with federal systems, in particular, provincial or state governments may have substantially more constitutional authority over land use than does the central government. Third, non-state groups also have deep territorial attachments and want to have authority over 'their' territory. In extreme cases, this can lead to separatism, a group's desire to form its own independent state. More interestingly from a conceptual point of view, non-state groups can exercise or push for forms of territorial authority that differ from the dominant understanding. Movements for indigenous self-determination within and across state borders are an extremely important example of this. It has been widely argued, too, that globalization is helping to replace modern territory with new, postmodern forms. These dynamics show that, while the dominant understanding is a central component of our territorial practices, we also need to be aware of the ways that reality often sits uneasily with, or flatly contradicts, ideas of linear borders, unitary sovereign authority and the state–nation connection.

Regulation refers in this book to the rules that people are meant to follow with regard to what they may, may not and must do with land. It also refers to the rules that specify how property is supposed to work: what kinds of rights people can have to land, who can have them and how they are to be recorded and enforced. There is an obvious overlap between the concepts of territory and regulation, given that a group that has authority over an area of land will also create and enforce regulations over it. Indeed, one of the core projects of states over the last two centuries has been the division of their land into zones that are regulated in different ways.[8] Most readers of this book will be familiar with the formal division of land between residential, industrial, commercial, agricultural, conservation and other uses, and with the idea that what can, cannot and must be done with land differs according to the way it is zoned. Someone living in a suburban residential area, for instance, might be obliged to keep their grass mown and forbidden from hanging their clothes outside to dry; they might be allowed to cut the trees on their property but be forbidden from operating a hog-fat rendering plant. Regulations might also prevent people from converting land from agricultural uses without permission, or make it difficult or impossible for non-citizens to buy any land at all (as we saw in Huang's saga). It should go without saying that regulations are not always followed.

While the connection between territory and regulation is deep, the overlap is not perfect for at least three reasons. First, some groups may feel an intense identity connection to an area of territory without having any practical ability to regulate land use there. The most obvious example of this involves people who have lost the land they consider their territory when it was seized from them by another group. Second, within states, the ability to regulate land is distributed both 'vertically', between levels of government, and 'horizontally', between different ministries and agencies at the same level. Within the state of California, for instance, a bewildering array of jurisdictions regulate different aspects of land use, including not only cities and counties but also districts in charge of fire prevention, flood control, parks and even mosquito abatement.[9] While this distribution is meant to correspond to different state functions and priorities, it may in practice lead to confusion and competition over just who is meant to regulate what where. In many countries in the South, horizontal and vertical regulatory competition is intense, there is extensive ambiguity over who has the formal authority to regulate which aspects of land use in what areas, and control over regulation in practice may bear little relation to what is envisaged in law.

Third, state agencies are not the only bodies that regulate land, and the regulations they do create are shaped by the influence of other organizations. Across much of the South in particular, village and neighbourhood groups and powerful local figures continue to regulate the use and the property characteristics of both rural and urban land. Regulations are also influenced, and in some cases created, by other non-state groups, including NGOs, private certifying bodies, and international organizations like UNESCO, the International Monetary Fund (IMF) and the World Bank. Influence is the more common dynamic and occurs when, for instance, NGOs push for stricter conservation measures and restrictions, the World Bank helps to rewrite property law, or the IMF pushes countries seeking funds from it to open up land sales to foreigners or to decentralize important land regulation functions from the national to local governments. Less common but still important are situations where international organizations and NGOs create their own rules for land use that states and other actors choose to respect, as happens when governments seek to have parts of their territory declared to be a UNESCO World Heritage Site or forestry companies seek sustainability certification for their operations from the Forest Stewardship Council.[10] I will pay special attention in this book to situations in which actors exercise sway over the regulation of land without seeking to acquire property or to claim any formal authority to rule over territory.

If regulation is the making of the rules regarding how land may, may not and must be used, *property* refers in this book to the right to make decisions about how a specific piece of land is in fact used within that structure of regulation. Many different kinds of rights are in play here, including the right of access to the land, the right to withdraw products from it, the right to decide how it will be used and managed, the right to exclude others from it, and the right to sell, lease or otherwise transfer rights to it.[11] As in the territory case, there is a dominant modern conception of property: private property, in which all of the rights to the land are held by the same entity. We usually conceive of private property as being held by individuals, families or private businesses, but in the sense used here it can also be held by states. Indeed, a very substantial proportion of the earth's surface is claimed by states as property – as Crown land, forest reserve, national parks, military bases and even as residential and industrial land. In some countries, all land is owned by the state. There is thus an important distinction to be made here between state claims to authority over land as territory, and the role of states and state agencies as property owners who may act as landlords in leasing land to private actors.

The last 500 years have witnessed a worldwide movement towards private property as the dominant form of property in land.[12] Within this broad trend, however, property rights continue to be defined and distributed in an almost infinite variety of ways. Many farmers in the South hold rights to use their land, to decide what to do with it, and to exclude others from it, but not to sell it. Agnes Varda explored a more circumscribed but still fascinating variation on full private property that continues to exist in France (and elsewhere) in her beautiful film *The Gleaners and I*: the right to glean, or to take what food remains after a crop has been harvested on someone else's private property. Property is also diverse, however, because of the tricky word 'rights' in our definition of the term. As noted above, across much of the world, multiple authorities – states and customary authorities in particular – claim the ability to decide which rights apply to any particular piece of land and who holds those rights. As multiple approaches to the regulation of property come into conflict, or as even relatively well-entrenched regulations are informally modified or set aside, property rights can become extremely unclear.

Several other points about property should be kept in mind. First, the various rights that go towards making up property can, again, be rented or leased. This point adds yet more complexity to the analysis of property, especially because the power relations in a rental arrangement can vary so spectacularly – from large landholders in poor, densely populated areas renting out land to desperate farmers at exorbitant rates, to transnational corporations, with state backing, leasing massive tracts of land in the South more or less for free. Second, billions of people around the world own enough land (for housing and for productive purposes) for it to make a difference to their lives, and billions more are able to access such land through the rental market. While land ownership almost everywhere is highly unequal (sometimes terribly so), and while enormous numbers of people are completely landless, land ownership is much more widely distributed than ownership of, say, timber or uranium. Finally, property in land (even when rental is included) is overwhelmingly national. As we will see in chapter 4, land ownership and rental by foreigners is very much the exception to the rule almost everywhere.

The plan of the book

What processes, then, are at the heart of the early twenty-first-century transnational politics of land? The rest of this book provides an answer to that question, with the relative emphasis on territory, regulation and property shifting as the book progresses. Chapters 2 and 3 deal primarily with geopolitics in examining two sides of the modern conception of state territory and borders. Chapter 2 takes up the 'external' side in tracing the historical and contemporary dynamics of a world in which all territory is assumed to be under the authority of one and only one sovereign state. It begins by tracing the emergence of modern international borders and the ways that territory has changed hands from state to state. Its central argument is that, while warfare between states constituted, until recently, a key mechanism of territorial redistribution, it no longer plays this role. This does not mean that territory is no longer disputed between states, and the chapter explores the nature of those disputes. It concludes by showing that many conflicts over territory lie outside the dominant modern conception of state territory. Chapter 3 examines the tension-filled 'internal' efforts of states to exert control over 'frontier' areas where their de facto writ is weak or absent. It considers 'the frontier' as a concept and the transnational relationships that often characterize frontiers, the importance of frontiers to the development of the global political economy over the last five hundred years, and the complex relationships between state officials, the people who live in frontier zones and other actors. It examines in some detail two parts of the world that are widely seen to be central to early twenty-first-century geopolitics: the Federally Administered Tribal Areas along Pakistan's border with Afghanistan; and the Canadian Arctic.

Chapters 4 and 5 focus on regulation and property in taking up transnational efforts to change the rules regarding how land is used, and who uses it, in the global South. The two chapters examine projects seen by their backers as being about *improvement*, about making land use more efficient, more profitable, more pro-poor and/or more sustainable. Chapter 4 shows that there has been a huge surge over the last fifteen years, and especially over the last five, in the transnational role in the acquisition – sometimes, but by no means always, by force – of land in the South for productive purposes. This land is usually first taken over by states in order to make it available to private actors (domestic or foreign) for large-scale agricultural projects and for non-agricultural uses such as industry, commerce, residential developments, infrastructure, and leisure and tourism. The transnational role in what has been dubbed a 'global land grab' is most obvious when foreign states and TNCs are among the actors acquiring the land, and indeed these actors have targeted many tens of millions of hectares of land in the South in recent years. Transnational actors have also, however, played a less direct but vital role in shaping the regulatory frameworks within which the land is acquired.

Chapter 5 discusses the enormous and highly detailed

interest that northern actors, especially states, international
financial institutions like the World Bank, and NGOs, have
taken in the way that land use is regulated in the South, and
the ways they have intervened to try to reshape it. It highlights
two key aspects of this concern: the regulation and administration of property rights (especially the provision of title to land),
which is purportedly central to economic development, and
the creation of conservationist regulations and specific conservation areas, which is supposed to protect the environment.
Finally, chapter 6 draws the themes of territory, property and
regulation together in taking up activism over land. It shows
how activism has become more transnational (especially in
the areas of indigenous and agrarian activism), but also analyses the fascinating dynamics of more localized activism in a
particularly important place (China's rural–urban fringe).

This book thus depicts a world in which diverse transnational dynamics permeate not just relations between states
and TNCs but also the way land is governed and conceptualized. This influence can play itself out even in the most
seemingly 'domestic' of situations. In stating that the above
processes are the key elements of the contemporary transnational politics of land, I do not necessarily suggest that they
are new. Some of these dynamics have existed for centuries,
though some of their current characteristics may be novel. It
is interesting to note, however, that some of the key trends
identified in the book – the near-disappearance of warfare as
a means of redistributing territory between states, intense
transnational interest in the conditions of land regulation in
the South, and transnational activism around land – date to
the 1970s, the decade often seen as marking the beginning
of the current era of globalization. I also do not suggest that
the dynamics I highlight are universal. Land politics cannot
be discussed only in the abstract, or as global trends. Their
many strands will always come together in a unique way in

any given area. I thus combine discussion of the big picture with studies of regions, countries and places. Such studies remind us that global trends do not simply beam themselves down into a specific locale; they show that people who seem to be in roughly similar positions in relation to these trends can respond to them in radically different ways – ways that run the gamut from uncompromising resistance to wholehearted and excited engagement.

'Land' is a complex and multifaceted topic. It is also huge. The focus on the transnational side of land relations in this book narrows things down somewhat. Even so, I have had to be selective in choosing what topics to address. I have, for instance, concentrated primarily on rural land, a choice that omits most of the world's most valuable land (in monetary terms, anyway) and that on which a rapidly growing percentage of the world's population lives. (The conversion of rural to urban land is, however, covered in chapters 4 and 6.) I also do not address the fascinating (and alarming) recent changes in the nature of international borders that highlight the ways states try to control access to national territory. I only briefly discuss mining and natural resource extraction, though these activities are among the most important reasons that TNCs seek control of land in other countries. Finally, and perhaps most importantly, the question of violent struggles between organized groups within states (including civil wars) that involve efforts to control territory, and the frequently critical transnational role in these conflicts, is addressed only obliquely in chapters 2 and 3. I hope that the analytical framework provided here will also prove useful in addressing questions such as these.

I would like to end with a word about concepts. As noted above, the definitions and proper use of many of my key terms – including territory, property, sovereignty, geopolitics, state, nation, war, transnational, frontier and social movement – are disputed in enormous academic literatures. (Interestingly, this is less true of the concept of 'land' itself.) A reasonably comprehensive discussion of the varying uses of even a couple of these terms would fill this book. While I highlight references in the footnotes and in the Selected Readings section for readers who would like to dig deeper, this book should not be treated as a fair introduction to scholarly work on any of these concepts. I have, instead, chosen my own definitions and proceeded with them. One consequence of this effort to keep things relatively unencumbered by scholarly scaffolding is that I have not always been able to acknowledge the parentage of the arguments I make. Finally, it is important to note that the distinctions I draw between my central concepts – territory, property and regulation – reflect a modern conception of the human relationship to land. These concepts, and the idea that they can be meaningfully distinguished from one another, have not necessarily been part of the mental furniture of all people at all times. I think that the concepts are useful in organizing our analysis, but they may obscure more than they reveal about other ways of being in the world.

CHAPTER TWO

Interstate Struggles

I begin this chapter with a familiar image. Political maps of the world show the division of the earth's land, as of 2012, between roughly 195 different states. Such maps indicate the inseparable connection between land and statehood in the modern world: a fundamental element of the definition of any state is the extent and location of its territory. The map's homogeneous colours and clear lines, too, graphically represent two bedrock modern assumptions about territory. Virtually all of the earth's land (outside Antarctica) is shown to be assigned to one, and only one, state; and states are separated by precise lines called borders (or by water). Comparing a 2012 world political map to one from 1912 would immediately reveal major differences, but they would primarily be ones of distribution rather than of kind. Different states existed then, the lines that separated them were in different places, and a small number of states had worldwide empires, but the two core assumptions about sovereignty and borders still apply across much of the map. In the tenth century, however, such a map would have been unthinkable. At that time, only a small fraction of the world's land unambiguously belonged to a single state, borders of the kind taken for granted today were unknown, and maps themselves, when they existed at all, were almost unrecognizably different to the ones in use today.

This is the first of two chapters dealing with the relationship between states and territory. This chapter takes up the 'external' geopolitical relationships between the states we see on the map, asking where the dominant modern conceptions of territory and borders have come from, how states have come to have the territory (the land) and borders they do, what are the key processes by which states gain territory from one another, and what kinds of disputes over territory exist between states today. The first section explores the emergence of the peculiar and historically unprecedented form of state territory that now defines international relations, and sketches the main processes – European state formation, colonialism and decolonization – through which states acquired and exchanged territory until the late twentieth century. The second – the core of the chapter – examines interstate war. It seeks to account for the striking changes in such wars in recent decades since 1945 and to explain why interstate war has more or less ceased to operate as a mechanism of formal territorial redistribution among states. The third section deals with territorial disputes, or situations in which states continue to disagree over what territory should be theirs and where their shared borders should be. The final section briefly highlights the exclusionary implications of the dominant assumption that sovereign states are the only legitimate territorial actors in international politics by focusing on situations in which these assumptions break down. Chapter 3 will take up the 'internal' side of modern state territory by examining how and why states try (or do not try) to impose their authority over their own territory.

This chapter raises some conceptual challenges.[1] It seeks to trace the history of how territory – land – has changed hands between states. The nature and definition of 'states', however, have themselves changed drastically over time. A critical change took place during the nineteenth century, when states became the only legal persons recognized as subjects under international law – the only organizations that can do things like declare war, sign treaties, join international organizations and claim territorial independence. Some of the attributes that it is now agreed an entity must have to be a state, like a permanent population, a government and territory, are characteristics of the entity itself. But 'stateness' also depends on whether or not the entity is recognized as a state by other states, and thus has a fundamentally relational (or social) element. In the nineteenth and early twentieth centuries especially, 'recognition' meant recognition by the European great powers (and, later in the period, by the United States). These powers recognized some entities – almost all of them European or European settler states – as 'civilized nations' to be treated as full states; recognized others, notably in Asia, as capable of engaging in international relations, even if they were insufficiently 'civilized' to count as fully sovereign; and withheld recognition from a very wide range of other territorial actors, including indigenous peoples. As discussed below (pp. 30–1), it was the process of decolonization after World War II that made the international society of states a truly global one.

Two things should thus be kept in mind about states. The first is that the category of 'state' and the international laws that buttress it have themselves been created by states and are in part the products of power and domination. It was the club of states – almost all of them, at the time, western – that determined that only states should be able to hold sovereign authority over territory. This exclusionary idea denies the possibility of sovereign territorial authority to, for instance, indigenous peoples, and also means that even some entities that have all the internal attributes of a state may not be recognized by other states (as illustrated by the case of Taiwan, taken up below, pp. 48–9). As the final section of this chapter argues, these groups are made invisible by the bold, confident colours on political maps; treating their claims as entirely 'internal' to states amounts to a refusal to listen to their voices. The second is that efforts to compare the ways in which territory has changed hands between states over a period of centuries encounter the problem that the further back we go in history, the fewer units involved in world politics match up with modern definitions of the state. Historical studies of warfare and territorial redistribution between 'states' will thus be strongly biased by the kinds of units they take to be states and the kinds of 'interstate' conflicts that their definitions make visible to them. According to the 'list of states in the international system' in the famous and widely used Correlates of War (COW) database, for instance, the world's only non-European state in 1816 was the United States, and China, usually seen as having been a state more or less continuously for the last two thousand years, did not become one until 1860.

Behind the map

The first key dynamic that has contributed to the nature and distribution of state territory today is European state formation. During the early modern period, a radically new conceptualization of territory emerged in Europe.[2] In the Middle Ages, the political space of the realm was understood as a collection of places, and its extent was represented not by means of graphical maps (which were exceedingly rare) but of textual lists. Realms also had blurry borders, with extensive frontier areas subject to unclear or overlapping jurisdiction. Even within core areas of the realm, sovereignty was distributed between types of actors and along complex, hierarchical chains of allegiance between people rather than concentrated in the ruler. The modern conception of territorial states that gradually supplanted these older understandings and representations between the sixteenth and early nineteenth centuries had two critical components. The first was the notion that all territory belonged to one and only one state. Ambiguous, hierarchical and spatially differentiated medieval ideas, in which sovereignty could be stronger, weaker, overlapping or non-existent, gave way to a homogenized conception in which every square centimetre of a state's territory was subject to exactly the same kind of sovereignty. The second was the linear border marking sovereignty's limits, limits which were precisely defined, surveyed and (ideally) recognized by other states.

This new conception of territory involved not just understandings but also representations of rule. It could not have come into existence without the remarkable developments in European mapping (including the universal grid of latitude and longitude) that were sparked by the early fifteenth-century translation of Ptolemy's *Geography* into Latin, or without the invention of the printing press that turned maps into mass-produced objects. Indeed, a strong case can be made that state territory was represented as homogeneous and linearly bounded on maps before it began to be treated as such in practice and in the conceptualizations of rulers. The new methods and maps made it possible for lines to divide even parts of the world that were largely unknown; an extremely important early example was the Treaty of Tordesillas in 1494, which divided the new world between Portugal and Spain along a line of demarcation running from pole to pole (though the precise location of the line was a subject of dispute). Negotiations between European states to define their mutual borders only picked up steam, however, in the eighteenth century, and it was not until the end of the Napoleonic Wars that the new territorial order was extended to all of Europe.

The ways in which territory changed hands between states also shifted during the early modern period. Before the Napoleonic Wars, sovereignty in Europe was largely held by dynastic rulers – literal sovereigns – as part of their personal patrimony. Territory could change hands in various ways, including warfare, inheritance, marriage, purchase and compensation. Charles V of Spain inherited a Europe-wide empire in 1519 as a result of the marriage alliances and patrimonies of his four grandparents. In the nineteenth century, however, sovereignty came to be associated with the people, the nation and the state itself. Nationalism in particular had profound, but complex and ambiguous, effects on Europe's borders. It encouraged a stronger emotional association between a state's people and its territory, and European rulers used official nationalism to try to deepen these attachments. But nationalism was also a force for the secession of nationally identified territories from larger states (as with Greece's independence from the Ottoman Empire) and for the creation of unified nation-states out of collections of smaller units (as with the creations of Germany and Italy). While nationalism redrew the territorial map of nineteenth- and twentieth-century Europe, the democratic idea that sovereignty inhered in the nation or in the people (not necessarily the same thing) meant that patrimonial practices of exchanging territory through inheritance or marriage became unthinkable.

Warfare as a means of redistributing territory, however, did not become an anachronism during the transition from dynastic to popular conceptions of sovereignty. War over territory was a legitimate element of European politics until at least the early twentieth century. One early twentieth-century international legal scholar stated that 'As long as a Law of Nations has been in existence, the states as well as the vast majority of writers have recognized subjugation as a mode of acquiring territory.' The legitimacy of this idea had come into question by World War I, as reflected in the ideas behind the post-war League of Nations, but World War II was very much a war of territorial aggrandizement on the part of Germany, Italy and Japan. In part (though by no means entirely) because of this bellicosity, the long-term trend until the end of the nineteenth century was towards a reduction in the number of states in Europe. Charles Tilly's much-quoted figures on this topic show both this consolidation and the difficulty of defining and counting historical 'states'. With respect to the year 1490, Tilly writes that 'No plausible set of definitions yields fewer than 80 distinct units or more than 500. We might arbitrarily take 200 as the median number.' Even in 1848, Tilly's range allows for between 20 and 100 states, but by 1890 (after the formation of Germany and Italy) the number is much clearer at around thirty.[3]

The second major historical dynamic is European imperialism and colonialism. Between the late fifteenth and the early twentieth centuries, European states (including Russia, and joined in the late nineteenth century by Japan) managed at one time or another to lay formal claim to the great majority of the world's land. One way in which they did this was through (almost always false) claims that the land was *terra nullius*, or belonging to no one. Warfare and purchase were also core strategies. The territorial side of European imperialism is not by any means a consistent story of the spread of modern territory and modern borders – nor would we expect it to be given that these did not exist in Europe at the beginning of the colonial era. The first centuries of colonialism were marked by a complex mix of forms of territory. Chartered companies like the British and Dutch East India Companies and the Hudson's Bay Company, for instance, controlled enormous amounts of territory as profit-making private entities licensed to use violence and to govern. During the nineteenth century, however, most colonies came to be claimed as sovereign territory by European states (though various forms of quasi-independence continued to exist) and acquired clearly drawn boundaries. It was also in the nineteenth and early twentieth centuries that the independent countries of Latin America and the states that had never been formally colonized – notably Japan, Siam/Thailand, Persia/Iran, Afghanistan and the Ottoman Empire/Turkey – moved towards modern borders.

The extent to which European conceptions of borders were novel outside Europe (as they once had been, of course, within it) is made wonderfully clear in Thongchai Winichakul's study of nineteenth-century British efforts to establish borders between their newly acquired colonies in Burma and in what is now Malaysia and the independent (and friendly) kingdom of Siam.[4] Thongchai shows that the Siamese conception of a 'boundary' in the early decades of this period differed from that of the British in many ways, of which I highlight five. First, for the Siamese, the demarcation of a boundary was not normally a job for the central authorities, but rather one that fell, to the extent that it fell to anyone, to people in the area. Second, the boundaries of two adjacent kingdoms did not necessarily touch. There could be substantial unclaimed areas of forest or mountains between them. Third, the locations of boundaries did not need to be negotiated or agreed with other countries, but could be extended unilaterally. Fourth, the boundary was not a continuous line, or even zone, but existed only where there were roads or passes used by travellers. There was no sense that it continued through, for instance, impassable mountains where no one would ever go. Finally, and perhaps most disturbingly from the point of view of drawing a linear border, it was possible for towns and even small kingdoms to be subject to hierarchical relations of authority with more than one ruler, and hence (from the European point of view) to be part of more than one state. All these ideas and more would need to change before Siam could acquire a modern territorial existence.

The third set of dynamics, those of the post-World War II period, has given rise to a remarkable increase in the number of states. While counts for the early 1900s vary between the low forties and the high fifties, as of June 2012 there were

193 members of the United Nations. These new states have largely emerged through three processes, all of which derive from the worldwide spread of nationalism and democratic ideas. They are: *decolonization*, the achievement of independence by formerly colonized states; *secession*, as new states break away from pre-existing ones; and *state break-up*, in which a state fissures into two or more new ones and the original state ceases to exist. Decolonization goes back to the late eighteenth- and early nineteenth-century revolutions in North and South America and in Haiti. Its heyday in Africa and Asia, however, encompassed the three decades after 1945. With decolonization largely complete by the late 1970s, the subsequent formation of new states has mainly been through secession and state break-up. Particularly notable have been the break-up of the Soviet Union and a series of secessions from Yugoslavia, which between them gave rise to at least 20 new states. Other secessions have included Bangladesh (from Pakistan in 1971), Eritrea (from Ethiopia in 1993), Timor-Leste (from Indonesia in 1999, though this could also be seen as a moment of decolonization), and South Sudan (from Sudan in 2011). Czechoslovakia broke up into the Czech Republic and Slovakia in 1993.

This proliferation of states since the early twentieth century suggests a geopolitical dynamic very different from the one Tilly highlights for sixteenth–nineteenth century Europe. World politics is sometimes seen as a highly competitive system in which the weak are conquered by the strong. Statesmen in late nineteenth-century Japan used the evocative phrase 'the weak are meat, the strong eat' (*jakuniku kyōshoku*) to describe this process. The twentieth-century record, however, suggests the opposite. While many new states have been created, few existing states have disappeared through violence since 1945. China took over Tibet in 1950 (though it had long claimed it); Indonesia invaded and annexed newly independent East Timor in 1975 (though, as noted above, this did not last); and North Vietnam conquered South Vietnam, again in 1975 (though this represented the culmination of a post-colonial struggle for national independence and reuni- fication, not some power-political calculation). States thus continue to die, as the USSR and Czechoslovakia demon- strate, but they seem no longer to be murdered. Similarly, while a highly competitive international system would pre- sumably encourage smaller states to amalgamate to better protect themselves and project power (along the lines of Italy and Germany in the nineteenth century), the post-World War II history here is distinctly underwhelming.

The end of interstate war over territory?

During the second half of the twentieth century, decoloni- zation, secession and state break-up saw new states emerge to take control over territory and establish (or affirm) their own borders. Within this broad trend, has territory – land – continued to change hands through warfare between states since World War II (which, of course, involved intense and far-reaching conflict over territory)? The question can be made more precise by splitting it into two: to what extent do states continue to *try* to take territory from one another by force; and to what extent are they *successful* in doing so? The difference can be seen by considering Iraq's failed 1990 attempt to con- quer Kuwait. Mark Zacher has compiled a list that seeks to show all interstate territorial aggressions between 1946 and 2000. For each conflict, Zacher gives the states involved, the beginning and end dates, the issue, the outcome and a clas- sification of the outcome as involving 'no change', 'minor change' or 'major change'. In Table 2.1, I divide Zacher's 40 cases by the decade in which he lists the conflict as having begun. The results are striking. States do continue to fight

Table 2.1 Results of interstate territorial aggressions, 1946–2000

	No Change	Minor Change	Major Change
1946–1949	0	0	2
1950s	2	2	0
1960s	6	1	5
1970s	6	1	5
1980s	3	1	0
1990s	6	0	0

Note: calculated from Marc Zacher (2001), 'The Territorial Integrity Norm: International Boundaries and the Use of Force', *International Organization* 55(2): 215–50.

over territory, with perhaps some sign that they are slowing down (three of the cases in the 1990s involve secessions from Yugoslavia). After the mid-1970s, however, efforts to seize territory stop being successful. With the exception of one case in the 1980s (a minor dispute between Mali and Burkina Faso that had existed since decolonization and was resolved by the International Court of Justice (ICJ)), Zacher's list shows no formal redistribution of territory resulting from international aggression after 1975. These two and a half decades are in stark contrast to the preceding three, during which there were four minor and twelve major redistributions.

Another remarkable element of Zacher's list is that very few of the attacking states are major powers in world politics and none are rich democracies. If territory is valuable to states, and if the most powerful states are most able to get their way, major powers could be expected to be the main aggressors. However, with the exception of the cases involving China and India between the 1950s and 1970s, none of the aggressing states can plausibly be described as major powers. The territorial aggressors between 1980 and 2000 were Argentina,

Ecuador, Eritrea, Iraq (twice), Libya, Mali and Yugoslavia (three times) – not exactly a who's who of geopolitical might. Similarly, the only example given of a major power being aggressed against is the (unsuccessful) Argentinian invasion of Malvinas/the Falkland Islands, a British territory 13,000 km from the UK. Other than this case, no rich democracy appears on the list in any capacity. Zacher argues that 'Wars of territorial aggrandizement since 1945 have, for the most part, concerned developing states' dissatisfaction with the boundaries they inherited from the colonial powers; but these quarrels are largely coming to an end.' Stephen Brooks, similarly, claims that 'concerns about territorial revisionism have essentially vanished among the most economically advanced countries.'[5]

The period since 1975 thus marks a dramatic change from that of 1945 to 1975, and an even more dramatic one from preceding centuries. Conflict over territory is usually seen to have been among the most important historical causes of warfare. Robert Gilpin, for instance, argues that 'Throughout history a principal objective of states has been the conquest of territory' and that 'states in all ages have sought to enlarge their control over territory and, by implication, their control over the international system.'[6] There are four broad types of reasons that might make taking control of territory seem appealing. *Security* motivations include controlling strategic pieces of territory, creating a buffer zone, controlling a sea lane and weakening or even absorbing an enemy. *Economic* motivations include the desire to control key resources (such as oil), to tax the seized territory's population and to integrate its economic production into the attacking state's economy. Considerations of *identity* include the argument that another state controls territory sacred to the attacker, or is oppressing co-nationals or co-ethnics. The final motivation is *glory* – the individual, institutional and national prestige that, in many societies, has come from conquering territory. While few readers of this book will live in societies that see seizing land by force as a source of status, the historical importance of this motivation should not be underestimated.

Given the power of these four motivations, the three findings noted above – that no interstate territorial aggression was successful between 1975 and 2000, that wars over territory are now initiated by relatively poor and weak states, and that major powers and rich democracies are no longer (with some ambiguous exceptions) the initiators or the objects of interstate territorial aggression – need to be explained. This necessity is deepened if land is also conceptualized as a resource. It is often argued that growing scarcity of key resources will lead to increasing conflict over them. While there is still roughly as much land in the world as ever, land is becoming scarcer in the sense that the world's population is growing while the land area is fixed. Yet the wars over territory that were once so common are now infrequent and, among rich democracies, obsolete. Why is that?

Much of the explanation lies in the fact that what is becoming less common is not just war over territory but interstate war in general. Analyses of war's prevalence, like efforts to determine the number of 'states' in the world, must make tricky judgement calls about what to count and how to count it, so there is some disagreement on this issue. With that in mind, I provide here some statistics on 'international war' from the *Human Security Report* of 2005. International war is a broader concept than interstate war; it includes, for instance, violent interventions by states against non-state actors in other countries. The war in Afghanistan is an international but not an interstate war, and the many wars of anti-colonial liberation also fit this definition. I use this measure here because it gives broader coverage than do measures of interstate war of state use of large-scale force across international borders.

The *Human Security Report 2005* figures for international war show remarkable recent declines. While the five-year moving average of international wars from 1816 to 2002 shows no clear trend up until the end of the 1970s, it shows a dramatic decline after that point, to the extent that such wars now barely occur. From the mid-1990s to the mid-2000s, 95 per cent of armed conflicts took place within, not between, states.[7]

The arguments I make to explain the decline in international war do not all address the same thing. Some deal with the general decline in war, some the absence of great power war since 1945, others the absence of war between democracies. They are also not necessarily competing explanations. Reduced warfare is most convincingly explained by the way these different forces interact with and reinforce one another. I begin with two explanations for the lack of war between the major powers since 1945. The first is the existence of nuclear weapons. It has long been argued that two states with second-strike capability will not go to war with each other. Such states inhabit a condition of 'mutually assured destruction' which is said to ensure that both will be obliterated by an all-out war between them. In the absence of any plausible route to victory, such states will do all they can to avoid direct conflict. This deterrence may also extend a 'nuclear umbrella' to allies and clients of states with second-strike capability. The second explanation, which arguably applies to the whole post-war period but becomes particularly powerful after the late 1980s, is the overwhelming military dominance of the United States. Because the US is much more powerful than not only any individual state but any plausible alliance of states fighting together, other countries should avoid going to war with it. The United States can hardly, however, be seen as a force for peace in general, given the large number of international wars it has initiated.

My next two arguments derive their logic from theories not

of *realpolitik* but of political liberalism. The third claims that democracies almost never fight one another. While a theoretical tangle hides behind this seemingly simple statement, proponents of the concept of the 'democratic peace' can point to the near-absence of wars between democracies as a basic empirical regularity of the last 200 years of world history. Fourth, international institutions have reduced incentives for war among states. The vast number of agreements, organizations, treaties and laws in which international relations have become embedded provide mechanisms for settling disputes that might once have led to war. Arguments about trade barriers can be taken to the World Trade Organization; those over maritime boundaries can be referred to the United Nations Convention on the Law of the Sea (UNCLOS); and those over sovereign debt repayment can be dealt with through the International Monetary Fund (rather than the old-fashioned method of gunboat diplomacy). The more states are enmeshed in these relationships, the more they stand to lose by jeopardizing their standing within them by embarking on unsanctioned wars.

Fifth and finally, changes in ideas and norms have reduced the incidence of war. One version of this argument is made by John Mueller, who argues that, like slavery and duelling before it, warfare has now come to be seen by large numbers of people as barbaric, anachronistic and repulsive. Because people no longer tolerate war, they will no longer support their leaders in engaging in it. A different, and to me more convincing, perspective claims not that people reject war, but that they no longer see it as glorious, as a source of social prestige for the individuals, institutions and states that engage in it. While individual wars may be seen as necessary and receive wide support, success in war is no longer a primary route to social status and the admiration of one's peers. In most of the world today, people who crave the limelight are better off becoming celebrities, business moguls or politicians than soldiers, and nations seeking prestige should look for it in the worlds of economics or sport rather than on the battlefield. (The extent to which this used to be otherwise is constantly impressed upon me by the fact that I live in Wellington County and work in Kitchener-Waterloo – names that honour two military leaders and a battle.) With warfare no longer an important route to status, a powerful incentive for individuals and states to engage in it has been removed.

These theoretical arguments need to be complemented by discussion of recent geopolitical developments that, as argued in the *Human Security Report 2005*, have been critical to the decline in international war since the late 1970s. The authors see this development – too abrupt, and extending to too wide a range of countries, to be fully explained by the forces canvassed above – as resulting from the disappearance of two major causes of war and the emergence of a new cause of peace. The defunct causes of war are decolonization and the Cold War, processes which between them were intimately linked to almost all international wars in the 1950s, 1960s and 1970s. The new cause of peace is the expansion of peace-keeping and peace-building activities, especially by the United Nations. The *Report* argues that these have played an under-appreciated role in bringing existing conflicts to an end, in preventing conflicts from reoccurring and in stopping the outbreak of new wars.

The above paragraphs have given theoretical and historical explanations for the decline in international war in general (over recent decades) and for the absence of interstate war between major powers (since 1945) and democracies (since the eighteenth century). Other factors help explain the decline in war over territory specifically. One is another shift in norms and ideas. Twentieth-century world politics saw the gradual emergence and institutionalization of a norm stating that changing international borders by violence – previously a normal and legitimate part of international relations – is unacceptable. Zacher has traced the development of the new norm in international treaties and charters such as the 1945 UN Charter, which states that 'All Members shall refrain in their international relations from the threat or use of force against the territorial integrity or political independence of any state'. This norm became well established for several reasons, some of them quite self-interested. Leaders of newly decolonized nations, for instance, used it to rally support (internal and external) against other states and nationalist movements seeking to challenge their state's borders. Indeed, respect for territorial integrity is not limited to relationships between existing states, but extends to the creation of new ones. Decolonized states have largely maintained the borders and territories bequeathed by their erstwhile rulers, while states emerging out of secession and state break-up usually inherit the pre-existing boundaries of sub-state administrative units within their former state.[8]

The last two centuries have also seen a halting and long-term, but profound, change in the relationship between territory, wealth and state power. Up until the eighteenth century, most state wealth ultimately derived from agrarian activities and was extracted from direct producers (such as peasants) by rulers with a political right to some of what was produced. In agrarian societies with slow rates of technological change, there was a close connection between a state's power and the amount of productive land it controlled, and a primary route to increased power was the conquest of territory. Two epochal transformations broke this connection. One was the industrial revolution. As it became possible to pack enormous amounts of industrial production into relatively small areas, states' wealth and population became decoupled from the extent of their territory, and rising productivity emerged as an alternative route to state wealth and power. This shift is visible in the land areas of the member states of the G8 group of major economies, which contains the three largest states by area (Russia, Canada and the United States), but also France (number 42), Japan (62), Germany (63), Italy (72), and the United Kingdom (80). (There is some dispute over whether the US is actually bigger than China; I treat them as tied for third place.)

The other major transformation was the rise of capitalism. As capitalist political economies began to appear (first in England by the seventeenth century, then elsewhere), politics and economics became separate spheres for the first time. In capitalist societies, states ruling over territory enforce the law and rights to property (including land) within their borders; that property is largely owned by private actors (individuals and corporations), which use it for productive purposes. States tax economic activity of various kinds, but the main mechanism through which the economic surplus is distributed becomes the market. If capitalist states do their job well and without too much regard to nationality, people and corporations from other states will be able to engage in economic activity within them, including the use of the land for agriculture, industrial production, real estate, mining, or what have you. Capitalism thus allows the ownership of land and rule over it – property and territory – to be fully separate. It also, of course, encourages trade as a means of acquiring goods from other countries. Foreign investment and trade allow capitalist political economies to derive profit and extract resources from the territory of other countries without controlling them politically. These dynamics make it possible to imagine a world composed entirely of capitalist states fully open to the international economy and providing full protection of property rights, a world in which market-based flows of trade, investment, finance and people would replace going to war for material gain.

The fact that these opportunities for peaceful economic interaction now exist does not mean that war is a thing of the past. As noted above, there are security, identity and status motivations for war in addition to economic ones. The existence of an alternative to territorial aggression also does not mean that that alternative will always be chosen. Powerful capitalist states continued to undertake wars of territorial aggrandizement against both their neighbours and potential colonies throughout the nineteenth century and the first half of the twentieth, and their motivations were at least in part economic. There are, however, reasons to think that, just as alternatives to war have emerged over the last two centuries, so territorial aggrandizement is becoming less appealing. Extracting economic benefit from conquered territory seems to be more difficult now than it was in the past (a phenomenon often referred to as 'decreasing returns to conquest').[9] Nationalism has made controlling foreign territory much more expensive and challenging than it once was. Suppressing movements for national independence requires enormous commitments of resources and human lives that will likely make conquest cost more than it is worth to the conqueror (though conquest may be highly profitable for specific groups within that state). The history of decolonization supports this argument, as does the recent experience of international quasi-occupation in Afghanistan and Iraq. Conquest is also discouraged by the complexity of key elements of the contemporary global political economy, notably those based on knowledge-intensive activities deeply interlinked through transnational production networks (see chapter 4). It is hard to imagine financial services industries, software development and just-in-time electronics manufacturing going on in territory under military occupation.

Another reason war persists in a capitalist world is that both the creation and the reproduction of such a world require force. Again and again over the course of the nineteenth and twentieth centuries, when powerful capitalist states have been denied access to coveted markets, trade, investment and resource extraction in other countries, they have used force to open those opportunities up. Their preferred method of doing this is crucial to the contemporary relationship between territory and interstate war. Rather than conquering and directly ruling territory, dominant capitalist states have sought to ensure (by force if necessary) that independent sovereign states maintain openness to the international economy. This argument about the 'imperialism of free trade' goes back to a 1953 article by John Gallagher and Ronald Robinson that claimed that, while Britain certainly engaged in formal conquest of territory during the nineteenth century, this route was, for British officials, very much a second-best outcome – indeed, a 'last resort'.[10] Far preferable was an *informal* imperialism in which local rulers would be forced to maintain key conditions for British investment and trade, such as free trade, protection for property rights and a functioning legal system, while also performing the onerous and expensive tasks of governing the territory, maintaining internal security, raising taxes and paying for defence. Britain's nineteenth-century relationships with independent Latin American states and with independent Siam provide examples of this dynamic.

The United States, however, has pursued the path of 'informal' imperialism much more consistently in the twentieth century than Britain did in the nineteenth. While the US has been unarguably the world's most powerful state since at least World War I, and while it has fought and won many wars over the last hundred years, the country's land area has barely changed since the 1870s (though the US did acquire and give up colonies during that period, notably the Philippines). Such a situation would have been inconceivable for a successful pre-capitalist empire in the days when benefiting economically from territory and controlling it politically were much more tightly linked. The American approach is illustrated by the 2003 invasion of Iraq. Precisely why the US attacked Iraq may never be properly straightened out. Almost no one, however, argues that the goal was to turn Iraq into a formal colony. Rather, the US moved with great speed to end the formal occupation and restore sovereignty to Iraq, a process completed by June 2004. At the same time, the US did all it could to ensure that the sovereign government would be open to international (particularly American) investment and oil extraction. It is partly in this context that we need to understand the efforts of the US and other capitalist powers to 'strengthen' weak states, a goal not just in Iraq and Afghanistan but in dozens of other countries. 'Strengthening' other states would make no sense if the plan was to take them over, but it makes perfect sense when the goal is for them to carry out tasks you want to see performed. Not all of these tasks involve protecting property rights and facilitating trade and investment, but some certainly do.

Territorial disputes

> Nothing can compensate the Syrian people for losing one inch in the Golan. Not even the moon.
> Walid al-Moualem, former Syrian Ambassador to the US, 1997[11]

To say that the world is now divided between sovereign states separated from one another by modern borders is not to say that there is one and only one universally recognized sovereign for every square centimetre of the earth's land. The confident lines and bold colours of a world political map paper over many disputes in which two (or more) states claim authority over the same territory. Territorial disputes can, of course, lead to war – indeed, it is widely argued that they are one of the most important reasons that wars break out – but they are consequential even when they do not. As always, how many disputes we see depends on how we define them. In this section, I do not consider as disputes cases in which states have not yet delimited (precisely specified) or demarcated (marked out on the ground) their shared border but have no particular conflict over it. I also stick to territorial disputes rather than arguments over maritime boundaries, though these can shape each other, as shown below. Even with these restrictions, my July 2012 reading of the list of international disputes in the CIA *World Factbook*[12] found close to ninety countries involved in at least one territorial dispute with another state. The list also shows that, while rich democracies may have just about ceased going to war over territory, they continue to dispute it: Canada, Denmark, France, Greece, Japan, Portugal, South Korea, Spain, the United Kingdom and the United States all appear. The most serious territorial disputes are among the most contentious and high-profile issues in world politics. Not all of them, however, are so intractable. Some are dormant; others are peacefully managed; and, as the CIA's list again shows, there is a steady process going on in which states, assisted at times by the ICJ, have been able to resolve their disputes.

In discussing these conflicts, I modify a typology used by Taylor Fravel to divide China's territorial disputes between those that involve *homeland, frontier* and *offshore* areas.[13] I define *homeland* disputes as those involving areas that are highly salient for at least one claimant because of the presence of substantial populations of co-ethnics and/or of historical associations taken to be important to national identity (battlefields, churches, supposed sites of a group's 'origins', etc.). *Frontiers* are discussed in more detail in chapter 3, but for now we can take these disputes to involve areas that are far from centres of power, close to other states and inhabited (often relatively sparsely) by ethnic minorities. *Offshore* disputes are over small islands, islets and rocks that are a substantial distance away from at least one of the claimant states. This is not an exhaustive typology when applied globally, and individual cases may straddle these categories, but it provides a useful basis for discussion. It is also important that not all territorial disputes are disputes over borders; those over island groups, for instance, do not usually involve the drawing of new land boundaries.

Homeland disputes tend to be intense. Deep associations between homeland territories and national identity make compromise extremely difficult and encourage protagonists to see the land in question as indivisible. While such associations emerge historically, rather than being objectively given, once they exist these disputes tend to become highly entrenched. Just to mention Ireland, Jerusalem, Kashmir and Kosovo is to give a sense of the intensity of such territorial conflicts and of their importance to world politics. *Frontier* disputes derive in part from the features of modern territorial politics. In the old days, there was no need for (or even conception of) precisely delimited borders in sparsely populated and often inaccessible frontier areas. Today, however, states are expected to have formally demarcated and mutually agreed borders, so things are harder to fudge. Frontier areas may not be seen as homelands, but that does not mean that they are not seen as important. They may be the location of important natural resources, or of strategic territory (such as mountain passes). The borderlands discussed in chapter 3 also tend to be the object of national security anxieties, precisely because they are close to other states. Frontiers will likely also be seen as part of the national territory and to be hung on to even in the absence of any other clear reason. Ron Hassner gives a sense of how such areas can seem intensely and surprisingly important:

In 1998 war erupted between Ethiopia and Eritrea over 250 square miles in the Badme region. The area is of no strategic importance and has no significant resources. Its population resides in a few hundred huts near a dirt track, growing sorghum and raising goats. Yet the dispute over Badme produced nearly 200,000 casualties between 1998 and 2004, and there is no peaceful resolution in sight. 'That area, I think, is desert,' commented one Ethiopian, but hastened to add: 'It's territory, you know . . . we'll die for our country.'[14]

Some *offshore* disputes are legacies of the colonial era. Many small islands around the world continue to be administered by former imperial powers, notably France and the UK, while also being claimed by nearby states. Other disputes involve tiny, and often even uninhabitable, (groups of) islands that were of little value before the advent of two developments. One of these is the technological ability to drill for oil and gas under the seabed. The other is the ability, under UNCLOS, for states to claim an Exclusive Economic Zone (EEZ) of up to 200 nautical miles from their coastline, and to receive sovereign rights to the resources in the water column and the seabed of their EEZ. Establishing maritime boundaries through the ambiguous UNCLOS demarcation process is difficult enough when the states involved have undisputed sovereign claims to their territory. In other cases, however, the territories that would form the basis for the claim are themselves in question.

The difficulties such situations entail are illustrated by the case of the Senkaku/Diaoyu Islands, a group of eight uninhabited islands in the East China Sea. These islands are disputed between China, Japan and Taiwan, but I focus on the China–Japan politics here. The islands had been sporadically visited by Chinese fishers for centuries before they were claimed as *terra nullius* by Japan in 1895. The United States took over their administration after World War II and formally returned them to Japan in 1972. Little interest was ever taken in them until reports in the late 1960s pointed to likely massive deposits of hydrocarbons in the surrounding seabed. Sovereignty over the islands has enormous implications for the location of the as-yet-undemarcated maritime boundary between China and Japan, and could give control of almost 20,000 square nautical miles of EEZ. Control over the islands has become one of the most difficult issues in Japan–China relations, with nationalist sentiment on both sides vehemently opposed to any form of compromise. No efforts have yet been made to take the dispute to international arbitration, for instance at the International Court of Justice, arguably because both sides have too much to lose, and it is unlikely that either side would respect a judgement against it in any case. Indeed, and ironically, international law arguably *heightens* this dispute between the world's second- and third-largest economic powers over a few square kilometres of rock, since both sides can appeal to international law principles to make their claim and since it is the potential EEZs under UNCLOS that make the land so valuable to begin with.[15]

Getting off the interstate

I have focused in this chapter on interstate relations over territory, or the 'external' side of dominant conceptions of state territory. This focus restricts the analysis to recognized states. Such states can be seen from one perspective as members of a club who have, between them, claimed exclusive sovereignty over virtually all of the earth's land. I have already shown that the emergence of this club over time (and through great violence) means that such a focus is a problem in historical terms. It remains a problem today. Many groups claim authority and sovereignty over territory in ways that reject the idea that their existence is entirely 'internal' to the territorial borders of a recognized state. I give two quite different examples. One is an entity that walks like a state, and quacks like a state, but is not a state: the Republic of China, which governs the island of Taiwan. The other is the treaty process between first nations and the federal and provincial governments in the Canadian province of British Columbia.

Many world political maps cheerfully show Taiwan to be part of China, and both the Chinese and Taiwanese governments agree with this assessment. What they disagree on is what that means. At the end of the civil war between the Chinese Communist Party and the Nationalists (*Guomindang*), the Communists had control over most of the mainland, which was constituted as the People's Republic of China (PRC) in 1949, while the retreating Nationalists moved the pre-existing government of the Republic of China (ROC) to Taiwan. Throughout the Cold War, both the PRC and ROC claimed to be the legitimate government of all of China. The ROC was recognized as such by many other states, and it held China's UN seat until 1971. Since then, however, the ROC – despite scoring well on almost all the attributes of 'stateness' – has been recognized by a dwindling number of quite small countries (23 by 2012), and in that sense has not really been a state. It is extraordinary enough that the PRC claims sovereignty over Taiwan, which has a democratic government, 23 million people and a wealthy, highly industrialized economy. But it is even more so that the ROC's Constitution formally claims sovereignty not only over China, which has 58 times its population and 267 times its surface area, but over former Chinese territory now claimed by, among other countries, Mongolia, Pakistan and Russia. Most remarkable of all, however, is that, while Taiwan has essentially recognized China's jurisdiction over the mainland since 1991, it is trapped in its state of constitutional chutzpah by the fact that the PRC would see any formal retraction of these territorial claims as a move towards declaring independence from China. That China would likely respond forcefully if Taiwan *stopped* claiming sovereignty over it must be one of the strangest situations in all of world politics.[16]

The second example derives from the history of first nations–settler land relations in British Columbia. British Columbia rejected the Canadian government's native land policies when it joined Confederation in 1871, and until recently refused to engage in treaty negotiations (including over land rights) with first nations. Aboriginal rights to land that precede European contact, however, gained new and much stronger recognition in Canadian jurisprudence and the Constitution during the 1970s and 1980s (including through the recognition of treaties as constitutional accords). Treaty negotiations were restarted in other parts of the country where treaties had not yet been signed and by the federal government in British Columbia, and the province eventually entered the process. The fact that many British Columbia first nations have not signed treaties and thus have not surrendered title to their land does not mean that their negotiations with the provincial and federal governments are 'interstate' in the sense used in this chapter – first nations mostly accept that they are part of Canada. However, the negotiations also have many features that make them hard to understand as purely 'domestic' in the standard international relations sense which takes states to have sole internal authority. The treaty signed in 1998 by the Nisga'a first nation, for instance, recognizes a form of 'citizenship' in the Nisga'a nation that includes a particular kind of relationship to Nisga'a territory. The Nisga'a also made their claims in the negotiations on the basis of their belonging to an independent political community that existed before the Canadian state and that possessed, in Carole Blackburn's words, rights that are 'inherent and temporally prior to the rights of nonaboriginal Canadians'.[17] This does not mean that first nations are 'states'. But it does mean that taking the treaty process to be a matter purely 'internal' to Canada means adopting a colonial approach to the question of territorial sovereignty. The issues of indigenous land rights and self-determination will be further discussed in chapters 3 and 6.

Conclusion

This chapter has investigated the nature and history of the modern conception of state territory and borders. It has asked how states came to acquire the territory – the land – and the borders that they have today, and how the mechanisms by which new states are born and land changes hands between states have changed over time. Inheritance, purchase and (more recently) formal colonization have disappeared as routes by which states can increase their territory, and many new states have, during the twentieth century, emerged to take control over territory through decolonization, secession and state break-up. War between states has not disappeared from the international system, but, after being one of the most important mechanisms of territorial and border change throughout history, it seems, since the mid-1970s, to have more or less ceased to operate for that purpose. I have identified the forces that generated this change. Some have been long-term, some much more recent; some have involved changes in norms, others the dynamics of international security, others the nature of capitalism as a form of political economy. I have also shown that the world implied by our maps – one in which all territorial claims and international borders are precisely specified and mutually agreed – has not arrived, and that disputes over territory continue to be a vital part of world politics. Finally, I have gone beyond the 'club' of states recognized by one another to show, through the cases of Taiwan and of first nations and Canada, situations in which the distinction between 'internal' and 'external' implied by modern conceptions of state territory fails.

The arguments in this chapter suggest a striking tension in modern ideas of territory. Territorial sovereignty and interstate borders have, particularly during the twentieth century, become more and more sacrosanct, to the point that efforts to change them by force are greeted with horror. The intense connection between national identity and land that so many people feel, too, suggests that there should be a strong resistance to foreign interference with the nation's land. At the same time, however, we are widely seen to be moving towards a 'borderless' world in which the lines on the map are not supposed to matter for flows of goods and investment (labour is a different story). Huang's saga gave an example of these tensions, which are enormously important in the global political economy, and many others will be given in the rest of this book. What is perhaps more surprising than these tensions, however, is how often they seem not to matter. It is, ultimately, the combination of the nation-state and capitalism, and the distinction this combination allows between territory and property, that creates the potential for this tension to be resolved.

CHAPTER THREE

Frontiers

Chapter 2 examined the 'external' side of the modern conception of state territory, the ways in which states relate to one another with respect to territory and borders. This chapter takes up the other side: the idea that states should have full control over their 'internal' territory, the land within their borders. I approach this question through the concept of the *frontier*. Like a number of the terms in this book, 'frontier' has been used to mean many things. The term as I use it has one essential characteristic and several common ones. The essential characteristic is that frontiers are areas where states fall well short of exercising administrative control. In frontier zones, states have great difficulty establishing effective governing structures, administering justice, collecting taxes and monitoring local activities. The state claim to be the sole authoritative source of law and government cannot convincingly be made of these areas. The flip side of this feature of frontiers is that non-state groups exercise some authority. Frontier land is contested as territory, and on the frontier the ability to rule on property claims and regulate land use is usually spread (often very confusingly) across different groups, including state agencies. 'Frontiers' are thus land over which states are internationally recognized to possess sovereign authority, but where they do not effectively carry out the administrative tasks of the modern state.

In many countries in the South in particular, this lack of effective state administrative capability can be a feature even of populous and accessible urban and agricultural areas. I use 'frontier' in this chapter to refer more specifically to areas that also have most, and sometimes all, of the following characteristics. Frontiers tend to be far from geographical centres of power. This distance may be a simple question of kilometres, but it can also be a feature of terrain like hills, mountains, swamps, deserts, forests and tundra where states find it difficult to maintain a presence, monitor behaviour and project power. Frontiers are often close to the 'edges' of the state, its borders and coasts. They are usually populated, relatively sparsely, by ethnic minorities. And they are often the recipients of temporary or permanent migration flows – sometimes very large and rapid ones – from other areas. Migrants move to the frontier for many reasons: to engage in ranching, in mining, or in forestry, to work for the military or to provide services for other migrants. From a land-use point of view, however, frontier migrations have been dominated by people looking to farm. Indeed, this movement of would-be farmers from more to less densely populated land has been one of the fundamental dynamics of the global political economy over the last 300 years. Global cropland expanded from, very roughly, 450 million hectares in 1700 to 1,800 million in 1990, and much of this expansion happened on frontiers.[1] The most famous of these movements, such as the migration of Europeans and Africans to the Americas, have been international, but domestic flows in countries like Brazil, China, Indonesia and Vietnam have also been massive and transformative. Migrations into areas already populated by different ethnic groups have led to conflicts (especially over land) ranging from low-scale tension to genocide.

The preceding paragraphs suggest a set of criteria according to which social scientists might objectively determine the 'frontierness' of a region (and indeed such indices have been developed). 'Frontierness', however, is an idea as much as it is an objective condition. Frontiers are imagined, and imagined in evocative ways; the Amazon, the Steppe, the Pampas, the Arctic and the Wild West are names to conjure with. Frontiers tend to be associated by people who live far from them (and by some who live within them) with a wide range of assumed characteristics: tradition, backwardness, underdevelopment, difference, inefficient and environmentally destructive resource use, indigeneity, rebelliousness, danger. These constructions have profoundly shaped state approaches to the frontier. The very notion of a 'frontier', too, is implicitly aligned with the perspectives of the state officials and migrants who want to deepen their presence in the region, rather than those of the people who have long lived there and for whom it is not a 'frontier' but home. It is also important that, just as state officials and majority populations imagine frontiers, so people on the frontier imagine the state, ascribing characteristics, objectives, capabilities and threats to 'it' that it may or may not possess. Oakley Hall's novel *Warlock*, a reimagination of the American legend of the Gunfight at the OK Corral, brilliantly conveys the ways that, from the frontier, the state seems at some times a present and compelling source of authority, but at others a distant, perverse, even absurd entity.

State officials worry about frontiers and seek to strengthen their control over frontier land for many reasons. They commonly express an obligation, even a mission, to extend the benefits of citizenship and development to frontier areas – to bring the benighted inhabitants of the frontier fully into the nation. Officials may worry that illicit activity of various kinds is going on at the frontier (they are usually right). Frontier concerns also have a strong geopolitical element. As rugged terrain far from the reach of state power, frontiers provide excellent bases for rebelling against the state and for groups causing problems for neighbouring states. The borders and edges of the national territory are also places where states are especially concerned with national defence. State officials also fret that territory that is not claimed with sufficient energy and clarity may fall prey to other states. All of the above concerns also relate to what James Scott has described as a powerful state drive to make territory 'legible', to be able to understand and to calculate what is taking place in the area under their rule, and the refractory characteristics of frontiers for these purposes are thus a source of frustration and a stimulus to action. Finally, while these points indicate the problems that frontiers pose to state officials, frontiers can also appear as solutions. Many states have sought to respond to demographic pressures in their core areas, and the threat of political unrest they carry, by encouraging, funding and organizing migration to the frontier. State officials may also seek to mobilize the resources and population of the frontier for the national economy (or, perhaps, for their own personal benefit) by extracting resources, encouraging industry and agriculture and levying taxes.

If the reasons state officials take an interest in frontiers are diverse, the ways that they try to exert control over them are equally so. State approaches can be usefully divided between the direct and the indirect. Most direct, and most obvious, are military campaigns that seek to subject territory and populations to state authority. States have put great emphasis on building transportation and communications networks in frontier regions, and a surprising amount of the history of roads, railways, telegraph offices and communications towers can be explained in terms of the internal state projection of power. States survey, map and gather information about frontiers. They try to extend the reach of state administrative agencies responsible for policing, education, border control, resource management and taxation. They try to stimulate economic development at the frontier through their own direct activity and/or by encouraging private corporations (including foreign ones) to engage in mineral extraction, agricultural development and industry. The ability of states to project power into the frontier in most of these ways has been transformed by advances in technology. The drone strikes and helicopter attacks being carried out by the United States in Afghanistan and Pakistan, the railway China has built through extremely forbidding terrain into Tibet, satellite surveillance of ice floes in the Arctic and of fires in the Amazon, and the use of GPS systems to collect many kinds of information just about everywhere all illustrate a spectacular increase in state abilities to know about and act at the frontier. Yet frontiers endure.

Two indirect aspects of state control over the frontier are of special importance. One is the common (though highly variegated) administrative framework of indirect rule. Under these arrangements, states do not fully extend the formal state administrative apparatus into the area. Rather, they work with and recognize as leaders people who usually have their own local bases of power that are somewhat independent of (though they may be enhanced by) their relationship to the state, and leave them substantial latitude to organize local affairs. Second, as noted above, states have very commonly encouraged migration to the frontier, especially by people from trusted ethnic groups interested in becoming farmers. Rodolphe De Koninck has enumerated the ways in which, in South-East Asia, peasants have served as 'the territorial spearhead of the state'.[2] Yet such moves are dangerous for states because migrants are also protagonists, people who do things that are forbidden, go where they are not supposed to go, get into fights with the people who are already living on the frontier (and with each other), and otherwise get out of control. They may also press the state to commit to the frontier resources it would rather devote to other things. One example of frontier migrants getting out of hand is what happened to the newly independent government of Mexico when, in the early 1820s, it encouraged migration to fill up its north-eastern frontier. After a few years under Mexican rule, these migrants, most of whom had come from the United States, decided that they would rather govern themselves and fought a war of independence to create the Republic of Texas.

Considering the relationship between direct and indirect state action on the frontier raises an important point about the 'state' itself. If we imagine 'the state' to be an anthropomorphized actor with desires and wishes, it is easy to assume that 'it' wants to fully assert 'its' control over the frontier – to be able to see everything, to know everything, to regulate everything, to extend the national administrative framework to every nook and cranny of the country's territory. If we think, instead, of actual state agencies (ministries, departments and agencies at different levels of government) and the actual people (bureaucrats and politicians) who occupy positions in the state, we are much more likely to notice the constraints under which they operate and the restrictions these place upon their goals. Frontier control is difficult and expensive, and may seem unappealing to agencies and people with limited budgets and other, more attractive priorities in less thinly populated, isolated, harsh, recalcitrant and unremunerative places. State agencies often discover, too, that among the biggest opponents of their frontier projects are other state agencies, whether because they balk at the cost or because they have their own goals for the territory. Finally, many local-level state officials at the frontier will often be from the area, and most will need to reach some kind of accommodation with local people in order to do any governing at all. State officials may thus be more attentive to local priorities than state dicta. If these cautionary notes apply to overly one-sided approaches to state goals, finally, we should also note that the responses of long-term frontier residents to state projects are not simply a matter of resistance and demands for autonomy. While such dynamics are usually important, people at the frontier often want things from the state, notably prosperity and modernity, and this can make their engagements with the state very complex. At times, indeed, they make impassioned pleas for *more* state activity in their area, pleas that the state may studiously ignore.

One last point about frontiers is that, while they are in one sense 'internal' to states, they are also areas where transnational dynamics can be powerful. When frontiers are also borderlands, the people there often lead transnational lives by engaging in cross-border trade, work and movement, and sharing social and family ties with people in the neighbouring state. Where frontiers contain valuable resources, they may be host to transnational corporations engaged in resource extraction. Such activities may raise concerns about sovereignty, but they can also be used to reinforce it. In the titling and conservation projects that we will examine in chapter 5, which often take place in frontier areas, transnational actors often work to increase the extent of state administrative control. Where frontiers are located at the 'edges' of states, finally, central authorities will likely be concerned about security both in terms of geopolitical challenges from other states and of the implications of illicit flows of goods and people across borders.

With all of this in mind, is there anything general to say about the ways in which control over territory is changing in the frontier regions of the world's states? There is something compelling about the argument that states are slowly, but inexorably, tightening their control over the surface of the earth, particularly when such arguments are applied to a long period of time and, as it were, from far enough away. Certainly states effectively control much more land in the early twenty-first century than they did in the early nineteenth. From closer up, however, the dynamics are more complex. In many parts of the South, state control has fallen off since the implementation in the 1980s of structural adjustment policies that directly attacked state capacity. Ongoing internal conflicts also attenuate state control. It is also important to be attentive to the many things that 'state' control can mean. It may involve top-down rule from the centre or the province/state, with standardized national frameworks imposed on people who have had no say in their creation; or it may involve the integration into formal structures of government of arrangements that leave much more room for self-governance and autonomy. Each frontier, ultimately, is different.

It is for that reason that I now turn to two detailed cases, each of which is widely seen to be central to the emerging geopolitics of the twenty-first century. In Pakistan's Federally Administered Tribal Areas (FATA), a mountainous region on the border with Afghanistan that has, since 2001, been a critical base for forces hostile to the foreign troops and new government in that country, the key issue is territory. FATA is caught up in a violent struggle for control and authority between a bewildering array of actors – Pakistan's army and Directorate for Inter-Service Intelligence (ISI), other state representatives, local leaders and tribes, insurgents, mullahs, political parties and the United States. (FATA, indeed, is sufficiently dangerous and difficult to access that contemporary on-the-ground research is scarce, and there are basic disagreements in the literature about what has happened there since 2001 in particular – something that should be kept in mind.) The extension of Pakistani state authority over this territory is widely seen to be vital for the national security not only of Afghanistan and Pakistan but of the US and the West. In the Canadian Arctic, the main actors are the Canadian government, the indigenous Inuit and transnational corporations, and the key concerns are Inuit land claims and political autonomy, Canadian sovereignty and resource development in a context of rapid climate change and disputes over the status of the Northwest Passage and maritime boundary claims in the Arctic Ocean. Territory, regulation and property are all in play, and a wide range of actions have been called for or undertaken by different groups on the grounds that they will 'strengthen' Canada's sovereignty in the area.

Pakistan's FATA

Most of the current geopolitical concern over 'frontier' conditions on Pakistan's side of the 2,600 km-long border it shares with Afghanistan focuses on FATA and the North-West Frontier Province (NWFP; see Figure 3.1).[3] The border here is the Durand Line, which was laid out by the British in 1893. The Line has never been viewed as authoritative by the Pashtuns (Pushtuns, Pakhtuns) who make up the majority of the population of FATA (including the 1.5 million refugees in the area at the end of the 2000s), the NWFP, and the adjacent parts of Afghanistan. Afghanistan has also refused to recognize the Durand Line since Pakistan's creation at the partition of India in 1947, and tried to prevent Pakistan's entry to the UN over this issue. The largely notional nature of the border is intensified by the extremely rugged, mountainous terrain through which it passes, terrain which poses a stiff challenge to external powers seeking to impose their will. Local livelihood patterns mostly ignore the border, which is criss-crossed by large numbers of small and more-or-less unmonitored mountain trails (though Pakistan claims to maintain around a thousand border posts on its side of the Line). Frontier conditions exist on both sides of the border.

External interest in the area that is now FATA has largely focused on geopolitics, security and territory; there has been much less state effort to regulate land use or take control of

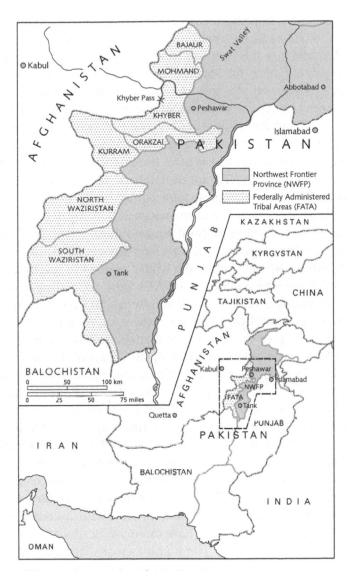

Note: The map does not show the six Frontier Regions.

Figure 3.1 Federally Administered Tribal Areas of Pakistan

property. It is important, however, to know something about social relations in the area (including those around land) to understand how the Pashtuns have engaged with state actors. The guiding ethos for Pashtun men is *Pakhtunwali*, a code which strongly emphasizes honour, reputation and personal autonomy.[4] One consequence of the code is intense male concern about controlling the behaviour of women in their families. Another is that the ownership of farmland is a core pillar of self-reliance and central to male social status. (The main land uses in FATA are pastoralism and agriculture.) A third is a deep unwillingness to recognize superiors or hierarchical social relations that expresses itself not only in relations with states but within Pashtun communities. *Pakhtunwali* is also accepting of violence, notably for purposes of revenge.

Frontier governance since the British period has specifically excluded the region that is now FATA from normal legal and administrative structures by institutionalizing indirect rule. Indeed, the formal governance structure in FATA is based to a startling degree on arrangements established by the British. FATA is made up of seven agencies (Bajaur, Mohmand, Khyber, Orakzai, Kurram, and North and South Waziristan) and six frontier regions (Bannu, Dera Ismail Khan, Kohat, Lakki, Peshawar and Tank). It is not governed as a province, but rather is subject to the executive authority of the president as exercised through the governor of the NWFP. The individual agencies are each administered by a political agent (PA) chosen by the governor, a position that goes back to colonial times. PAs recognize tribal leaders (*maliks*) as local interlocutors and reward them for maintaining order with discretionary funds and other perks. PAs have extensive flexibility in their relations with the tribes. The highly personalistic and informal rule they exercise resembles a system of alliance-building and bribery rather than one of administration, and leaves the tribes extensive authority to run their own affairs.

This freedom, however, is circumscribed by the Frontier Crimes Regulations (FCR), which continue to apply in FATA more or less as last revised by the British in 1901. The FCR encourage PAs to refer civil and criminal disputes to tribal councils (*jirga*) for resolution, and thus to some degree defer to tribal autonomy – though the PA can appoint the *jirga* and decides whether or not to accept its verdict. The FCR also, however, give PAs wide-ranging and arbitrary power to use measures like preventive detention, collective punishment, seizure of property and economic blockades against tribes. The FCR place the residents of FATA outside the jurisdiction of Pakistan's courts, and indeed deny them the basic civil rights of Pakistani citizenship, including the right to legal representation. On the political side, while FATA does have representation in the national parliament, political parties are banned. Members of the National Assembly from FATA were chosen by an electoral college of *maliks* until the 1997 elections, when full adult franchise was finally granted. The political and judicial structures of FATA place the region in a colonial relationship to the national state, and pressure for reform of the administrative set-up and the FCR is building in Pakistan. It is not clear what the relevance of such reform would be in practice, however, given that this system of governance is, as we will see, already effectively defunct across wide swaths of FATA.

Where did this system come from? The British approach to the North-West Frontier derived from the fact that the area was of concern to the East India Company and, after 1858, the government of India not for economic but for security reasons. Worries about the southward extension of Russian power, in particular, meant that the frontier mountains were seen as a critical line of defence. Neither the company nor the government, however, ever tried to impose full administrative control in the area. Rather, the British approach to the region took on the form of what Lord Curzon would, in the early twentieth century, call the 'threefold frontier'. The innermost frontier was (quoting Ainslee T. Embree) 'the administrative boundary up to which the Government of India exercised its full authority'; the second was 'a zone claimed as Indian territory, in which the government made no attempt to impose its laws or political jurisdiction, but permitted tribal chieftains to order their own affairs' up to a clearly demarcated international border; and the third was made up of independent protectorates (like Afghanistan) tied to the government of India by treaties.[5] The British took this approach for several reasons. Directly controlling the region was not worth, in economic terms, what it would cost. The British also saw the Pashtuns as too proud and martial in spirit to be conquered, and worried that any effort to rule them directly would only push them into the arms of foreign powers. This aspect of British policy also had a principled side that drew on conservative arguments for the preservation of 'ancient' constitutions and traditions. Rather than trying to bring the frontier under formal administration, then, the British invested substantial discretionary power in their representatives in the area, creating a personalistic and unstructured form of rule which sought to maintain alliances with the tribes (including by making direct payments to them) while also mounting frequent punitive expeditions to deal with activities beyond the limits of British tolerance.

Independence in 1947 brought surprisingly little change in relations between the central state and the frontier. While the Indian Independence Act cancelled the treaties the British had signed with the tribes, the same basic relationship was reconstituted by the tribes and by Pakistan's first Governor-General Mohammad Ali Jinnah, who had promised at independence to respect tribal autonomy. The most fundamental change was demilitarization; after a century of constant British military expeditions, the army withdrew from FATA in 1947 and did not return until 2002. However, the state, and especially the army, did seek to use FATA to exert influence in Afghanistan. Between the 1950s and the 1970s, Afghan governments promoted the idea of an independent Pashtunistan state for the region as a means to pressure Pakistan, and much Pakistani frontier policy aimed at combating this idea. From the 1970s, a key element of this policy was the promotion of Islamist groups and mullahs (clerics) as a counter to pan-Pashtun nationalism. This approach intensified (even as the idea of Pashtunistan withered) after the Soviet invasion of Afghanistan in 1979, as FATA became the critical base for the *mujahideen* groups that fought the Soviets with Pakistani, Saudi and American support. It continued, moreover, through the 1990s, when Pakistan's army and Inter-Service Intelligence supported the (largely Pashtun) Taliban movement in Afghanistan, and (more controversially) the 2000s, when concerns about Indian influence in post-Taliban Afghanistan and about the prospect of a power vacuum if NATO forces were to withdraw led the army and ISI to keep supporting the Taliban while claiming to oppose it. More or less since independence, then, the army and ISI have appreciated the free hand they are given in FATA by the exclusion there of normal governance structures. In the Pakistani as in the British period, while key state agencies take great interest in the frontier, they seem reluctant to extend what is often called 'the writ of the state' there.

The colonial governance structure in FATA came under severe pressure in the 1980s and 1990s. As money, weapons, ideas, and people (both *mujahideen* from across the Islamic world and Afghan refugees) poured into FATA in the 1980s, long-standing political relations began to fray. Mullahs had never had much independent power in the frontier areas, but they gained authority during the 1980s from the support of both Pakistan and the *mujahideen*, authority that came at the expense of the *maliks* and other tribal elders. FATA's economy was also transformed as long-standing pastoral and agricultural pursuits were overshadowed by huge flows of external cash, new cross-border markets for drugs, weapons, and smuggled goods, and remittances from the Pashtuns who were working in increasing numbers in other parts of Pakistan and in the Middle East. These flows of money had their own impact on local governance, as *jirga* decisions came increasingly to be swayed by payments.[6]

FATA was thus undergoing profound social, political and economic change even before the United States attacked Afghanistan in conjunction with local anti-Taliban forces in late 2001. As the Taliban government fell, Taliban and al-Qaeda-affiliated fighters crossed the border, seeking refuge in FATA. In response, and as a result of American pressure to capture al-Qaeda members, the Pakistani army began moving into FATA from 2002. These movements involved attacks not just on the newly arrived fugitives but on some of the area's Pashtun tribes. The pattern of army activity is generally described as an oscillation between the heavy-handed use of force (with substantial civilian casualties) and the signing of 'peace deals' when military operations prove unsuccessful. This effective invasion led more and more Pashtuns in FATA and the NWFP to take up arms in what became something between an insurgency and a civil war. By mid-decade, the influence of what Joshua T. White calls 'neo-Taliban insurgents' was spreading rapidly through FATA and even extending to 'settled' areas of the NWFP. By the end of the decade, roughly one third of the population of FATA had been displaced by the fighting.[7]

Events since 2001 have accelerated the breakdown of the old governance structure in FATA. The declining power of the *maliks* is graphically illustrated by estimates that hundreds have been assassinated since 2002, and even where *jirgas* under the old arrangements continue to function, they now face constant intimidation from insurgents. The old regime, and especially the role of the PAs, has also been undermined by the government. As the army became the major state force in FATA after 2002, the PAs were deliberately swept aside in favour of army officers as the main points of contact with the tribes. PAs do, however, continue to maintain some power as a result of their control over agency development funds, and they have continued to use the FCR's collective punishment regulations (including the detention of women and children) against tribes accused of harbouring foreign fighters. Efforts at formal governance reform, including the creation of a new secretariat for FATA in 2002 and the 2001 implementation of the Local Government Ordinance in the settled areas of the NWFP, have also had unanticipated and destabilizing consequences.[8] FATA has become subject to a spatially differentiated, shifting and violent mix of influence and control involving the Taliban and Taliban-affiliated forces, mullahs, PAs and the army.

The final central element of FATA's current trajectory is the strong interest external actors, and especially the United States, take in the region. Pakistan's tenuous authority in FATA (a region described by George W. Bush as 'wilder than the Wild West') is widely viewed in the West as one of the major problems of world politics, and by foreign policy-makers in the US as one of the most critical threats to American national security. (It is worth taking a moment to appreciate how remarkable it is that the world's sole superpower, located quite literally on the other side of the planet, should feel so threatened by such an impoverished area.) The US has thus tried, as it has in many other countries in which it has intervened militarily since World War II, to support the extension of state authority into the frontier. Part of the

American strategy has involved support for standard methods of frontier control. In March 2007, the US promised to spend US$750 million on development in FATA over five years. The American bilateral development agency USAID, for instance, is funding the construction of two 100-km roads from the city of Tank into South Waziristan, a move meant to increase economic opportunities and stimulate investment.[9]

American policy towards the Pakistani state's position in the frontier, however, is not entirely supportive. Since 2006–7, American officials have vocally questioned which side Pakistan is really on in the 'war on terror'. They have also emphasized that the war in Afghanistan cannot be won without the elimination of the sanctuaries that forces opposed to the Afghan government enjoy in FATA, and have pressured the Pakistani state to bring FATA and the NWFP more firmly under its control. The US has also, however, insisted on acting independently within sovereign Pakistani territory. American missile strikes from drones, despised in Pakistan and publicly opposed by the government, are a constant reminder of this, but the most spectacular instance to date has of course been the May 2011 raid to assassinate Osama bin Laden in Abbottabad in the NWFP. Pakistan was informed of the raid only after the fact. The American approach, which demands that Pakistan take up full sovereignty over FATA while refusing to respect that sovereignty, is thus deeply contradictory.

A deeper tension involves the question of whether Pakistan should even be trying to extend 'the writ of the state' in FATA. For some analysts, such moves represent the indispensable precondition for any positive developments in FATA. As long as the people of the area are excluded from the civil and political benefits of Pakistani citizenship, they argue, and as long as the army and ISI can act with impunity in the region, settlement of the conflict is impossible. Democratization and the extension of the rule of law into FATA are thus the solution to the problem. For other observers, though, state presence in FATA is not the solution but actually a major part of the problem. Those who emphasize *Pakhtunwali* in particular are likely to see the Pashtuns as fundamentally ungovernable and as determined to resist any effort by outside agencies to order their affairs.

The Canadian Arctic

Challenges to state territorial control in the Canadian Arctic are particularly striking. Definitions of the Arctic differ, but the focus here will be on the northern parts of what are now the Canadian jurisdictions of the Yukon, the Northwest Territories, Nunavut, Quebec, and Newfoundland and Labrador (see Figure 3.2).[10] This territory is divided between the northern parts of the North American mainland and the Arctic Islands, which stretch as far as 84 degrees north. The Arctic climate is forbiddingly cold for much of the year, the land is largely tundra, and the potential for agriculture is limited at best. Sea ice covers much of the Arctic Ocean and the waters between the islands, with its extent waxing in the winter and waning (by the early 2010s, waning dramatically) in the summer. The further north one goes within the Arctic Circle, too, the more the year is divided between periods of constant daylight in the summer and constant darkness or twilight in the winter. The challenges the Arctic poses to human habitation are well illustrated by the fact that in 2011 Nunavut, which accounts for one fifth of Canada's land and is larger than Mexico, had a population of 33,413 and a population density of 0.016 people per km^2.

The indigenous inhabitants of the Canadian Arctic are the Inuit, a circumpolar people living in what are now eastern Russia, Alaska, northern Canada and Greenland. When post-Norse European exploration of the Arctic began in the 1500s,

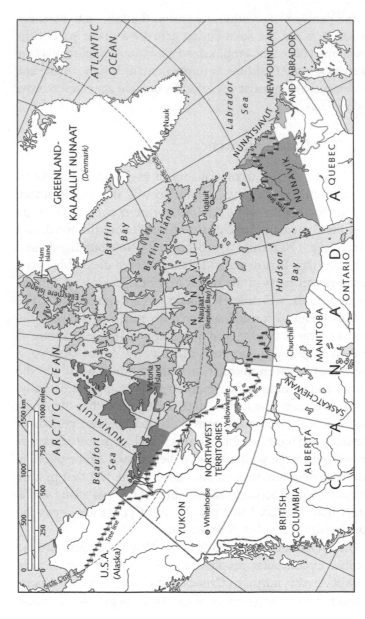

Figure 3.2 The Canadian Arctic

Inuit livelihoods were based on hunting. The European presence in the Arctic was minor until the nineteenth century, but Inuit contact with whalers, traders, and missionaries transformed their lives through, for instance, wider participation in non-subsistence-oriented hunting and the introduction of rifles and new diseases. The Canadian government received its Arctic lands in two chunks: a massive area previously held by the Hudson's Bay Company was purchased in 1870, and Britain transferred its (rather tenuous) sovereign claim to the Arctic Islands to Canada in 1880. Canada at this time had virtually no capacity to assert its sovereignty in the Arctic (in the late nineteenth century, the country lacked a navy of any kind, let alone ships that could deal with sea ice). Enthusiasm about changing this situation was dampened by the expense and difficulty of maintaining an Arctic presence and the perception that the region was largely worthless economically.

The government slowly began to pay attention to the Arctic in the early twentieth century. The 1920s, in particular, saw the extension of a police presence, an effort to bring Canadian law to the Arctic and relocations of Inuit to uninhabited areas further north. Moves like these were motivated by the goal of establishing Canada's 'effective occupation' of the Arctic, something seen as critical to supporting the country's sovereignty claims. During this period, however, Canada took essentially no responsibility for the Inuit, who never signed a treaty and were not brought under the Indian Act. While sovereignty over the Arctic Islands was something of a point of tension with the US and Norway in the early twentieth century, these disputes were resolved by the early 1930s. Since then, Canada's only Arctic territorial dispute has been an as yet unresolved conflict with Denmark over Hans Island, a 1.3 km^2 pile of rock between Greenland and northern Ellesmere Island.

World War II and the Cold War transformed the Canadian

government's attitude to the Arctic. There was a massive American military and civilian presence in the region during World War II (with American personnel outnumbering Canadians), and concerns about a Soviet attack led to a large continuing presence after it. While the Americans did not dispute Canada's claim to the region, the scope of their activities and the fact that they were largely responsible for Canada's northern defence led to worries about damage to de facto Canadian sovereignty. Americans, too, were critical of Inuit living conditions and the lack of Canadian efforts to better their situation.

This, combined with the development of a Canadian welfare state after the war, led to what Frances Abele and Thierry Rodon call a 'rapid incursion into the north of a newly vigorous state presence'.[11] The government began to extend education, health care and economic development programmes into the Arctic, and to build housing meant to prompt the Inuit to settle in permanent communities. While the government had, until World War II, encouraged the Inuit to persist with their traditional way of life, it now sought to help them become wage earners. This more proactive stance led to some tragic outcomes, including the creation of residential schools at which Inuit children were separated from their parents, forbidden to speak their own language and often abused, and to further relocation projects that went badly wrong. The government's new preoccupation with intervening in Inuit lives and with 'legibility' in the Arctic is well illustrated by the 'E-number' discs (with 'E' standing for 'Eskimo') that the Inuit were meant to wear and needed to show as proof of identity in their dealings with the state. E-numbers were in use from the early 1940s to the early 1970s, but were then replaced by 'Project Surname', an effort by the Northwest Territories Council to get all Inuit to choose family names with standardized spellings.[12] Behind much of this new activity was the idea that the government needed to extend the normal benefits of Canadian citizenship to the inhabitants of the Arctic if it was to claim 'effective sovereignty' over it.

If the 1950s and 1960s were largely characterized by the top-down imposition of Canadian government programmes in the Arctic, the 1970s saw the beginnings of a very different form of politics. As the push for natural resources development in Alaska and northern Canada gathered steam in the late 1960s, the Inuit began to mobilize politically, both out of concern over the potential negative impacts of the projects and to argue that they should share in the benefits of resource development on what they saw as their land. Some of this new political activity took place transnationally through the formation of the Inuit Circumpolar Conference (later Council), a remarkable organization that brings together Inuit from the US, Canada, Greenland and Russia and that has come to play a key role in Arctic diplomacy.

Within Canada, Inuit organizations pressed the federal and (in Quebec and Newfoundland and Labrador) provincial governments to settle land claims. Final land-claim settlements were reached for Inuvialuit in 1984, Nunavut in 1993, Nunatsiavut in 2004 and Nunavik in 2006 (see Figure 3.2). These agreements saw the Inuit receive title to specified areas of land (with sub-surface rights to smaller amounts), cash payments and the right to participate in co-management of certain wildlife and environmental issues. In exchange, the Inuit gave up their claims to the remaining lands within the settlement area. Inuit groups across the Arctic thus now own large areas of land and water (some of which were chosen specifically for their resource development potential) and have influence (but not decision-making power) over some issues of wildlife and environmental regulation on the rest of the land. The land-claim settlement process also led to new forms of self-government in all four areas. The most striking result of these has been Nunavut, a new territory created out of almost 2 million km² of land from the Northwest Territories in 1999. The Nunavut government is a 'public' one that represents all the people of the territory, but the Inuit make up about 85 per cent of the territorial population. The land-claim settlements and new forms of self-government mean that Inuit are now both the owners of extensive land and resources as property, and formal participants in some resource and environmental regulation. The federal government, however, still holds jurisdiction over lands and resources in the Northwest Territories and Nunavut, authority it has been unwilling to devolve to the territorial governments.

The period from the late 1960s also saw substantial action over Canada's claims to the waters within the Arctic Archipelago. Canada has long claimed that these waters, including the Northwest Passage that links the Labrador and Beaufort Seas and thus the Atlantic and Pacific Oceans, are internal waters subject under international law to the same kind of sovereign authority as national territory. The United States disagrees, arguing that the Northwest Passage is an 'international strait' through which its vessels (and those of other countries) are free to pass. This difference was brought to a head by southern Canadian reactions to the 1969 voyage of Humble Oil's *SS Manhattan* through the Northwest Passage, and again in 1985 by the transit of the US Coast Guard icebreaker *Polar Sea*. In the former case, Canadian responses included the assertion, through the 1970 Arctic Waters Pollution Prevention Act, of the right to apply anti-pollution regulation within a zone of 100 nautical miles from the coast. In 1986, meanwhile, Canada officially drew 'baselines' around the Archipelago under UNCLOS rules and formally declared all waters within them to be internal.

While these disputes were seemingly over water, Canada's case engaged in some creative reconceptualization by arguing that historical Inuit use of sea ice did not differentiate between land and sea. As Secretary of State for External Affairs Joe Clark put it in 1985, 'Canada's sovereignty in the Arctic is indivisible. It embraces land, sea and ice. [. . .] From time immemorial Canada's Inuit have used and occupied the ice as they have used and occupied the land.'[13] This Canadian position on sea ice calls into question the usual assumption, discussed in chapter 1, that the world's surface is divided between only land and water, and seeks to introduce a third category into international debates over sovereignty. The argument that Inuit occupation 'from time immemorial' is at the base of Canada's claim to the Arctic sea ice also sits awkwardly, of course, with the fact that Canada received its claim to the Arctic Islands from Britain, which had originally claimed them as *terra nullius* (land belonging to no one).

It is not clear what would happen to this argument if the ice were to disappear. During the 2000s, the Arctic was thrust onto the front pages of the world's newspapers by two momentous developments. One was a dramatic increase in natural resource prices (see chapter 4). The other was the rapid decline in sea ice cover during the Arctic summer, a trend that has left scientists scrambling to figure out why the ice is retreating so much faster than climate change models had predicted. The natural resources of the Arctic land and seabed are becoming more attractive as objects of exploitation just as warmer temperatures and melting ice are facilitating access to them. Disappearing sea ice also makes the Northwest Passage more viable as a shipping route that takes 7,000 km off the trip from Europe to Asia. As the new appeal of Arctic resources heats up pre-existing disputes over the boundaries of Exclusive Economic Zones and extended continental shelf claims between the region's states, many commentators have argued that the Arctic will be one of the key points of conflict in twenty-first-century geopolitics. While disputes over maritime boundaries in themselves are outside the scope of this book, it is important to examine how arguments over maritime claims motivate actions on land. Both the Canadian government and the Inuit argue that Canadian sovereignty in the Arctic is incomplete in a way that threatens Canadian claims there. While their positions are quite different in key respects, they also show areas of commonality that point to a novel conception of sovereignty in the Arctic.

Since coming to power in 2006, Canada's Conservative government, and especially Prime Minister Stephen Harper, have put strong emphasis on Arctic sovereignty. While Harper, who makes an official visit to the Arctic every summer, has gone so far as to suggest that Canada's 'territorial integrity in the Arctic' is under threat, most government and Conservative Party statements refer to vaguer concerns. The following quotation is characteristic: 'Canada has a choice when it comes to defending our sovereignty over the Arctic. We either use it or lose it. And, make no mistake, this Government intends to use it. Because Canada's Arctic is central to our identity as a northern nation. It is part of our history. And it represents the tremendous potential of our future.' The Conservative policy approach to 'using' the Arctic has prioritized the holding of military exercises in the region and announcements of big-ticket items like patrol ships and a deepwater harbour for Iqaluit, though few of these promises have materialized to date (and the harbour has been cancelled). Whether governmental priorities for the Arctic will translate into budgetary approvals remains to be seen. Harper has also been criticized for greatly exaggerating threats to Canada's Arctic sovereignty as a means of winning southern votes. It is interesting to note in the context of the resource rush, too, that the nationalist stance being taken towards the Arctic need not imply that the 'using' must be by Canadians. Foreign companies extracting resources also help protect sovereignty if they recognize the authority of, and are regulated by, Canadian governments. In May 2011, for instance, the provincial government of Quebec launched a plan to promote resource development and tourism in northern Quebec that included a campaign to attract foreign investment. Quebec Premier Jean Charest explicitly linked the project to Canada's disputed claim to the Northwest Passage, and stated that the plan 'is an affirmation of sovereignty, and we are very, very conscious of the fact that we need to occupy our territory'.[14]

Inuit groups, unsurprisingly, have not appreciated these claims that the Arctic is not being 'used'. Inuit leaders have consistently taken the position that they are proud Canadian citizens willing to work with the government to strengthen Canada's sovereignty claims; they have not, unlike the Inuit in Greenland or the Innu in Labrador, pushed for independence or full sovereignty. However, their emphasis in sovereignty debates has been quite different from, and has at times contradicted, that of the federal government. The Inuit have opposed the idea that protecting Canadian sovereignty in the Arctic requires further militarization of the region. They have supported natural resources development, but want both to benefit from it and to have a say in regulating it. While the land-claim settlements and self-government arrangements have made a start in this direction, the government of Nunavut has pushed for further devolution of jurisdiction over land and resources (and the receipt of royalty payments for them) from the federal to the territorial level, and negotiations over this are ongoing.

The Inuit have also strongly emphasized the argument that Canada's sovereignty is tied to their socio-economic development. As Mary Simon, the past president of Inuit Tapiriit Kanatami (Canada's national Inuit organization), has put it, 'For Canada to assert its sovereignty legitimately in the Arctic, it must also ensure that Inuit are treated as all other

Canadians are . . . with the same standard of education, health care, and infrastructure that is the foundation of healthy communities across Canada.' Canada's Arctic sovereignty thus needs, she argues, to be underpinned by 'viable and healthy communities, sound civil administration, and responsible environmental management . . . not just ports, training facilities, and military exercises.' Inuit representatives have at times claimed that the nature of Canadian policy towards the Arctic and the Inuit is a threat to international recognition of Canada's sovereignty. Former Nunavut premier Paul Okalik, for instance, argued in 2005 that the territory's lack of control over the 'internal' waters of the Archipelago – jurisdiction Nunavut would have if it was a province – was an example of Nunavut being treated as a 'colony' on the 'national stage', and asked 'If Canada treats Nunavut like a colony or some "off-shore" territory, is it any wonder that other countries do the same?'[15]

While Inuit and Canadian government approaches to Arctic sovereignty thus have fundamental tensions, there are also some interesting commonalities that point to the emergence of new conceptions of sovereignty. In arguing, for instance, that Canada's sovereignty in the Arctic clearly exists but also needs to be 'strengthened', both sides imply that sovereignty is not an either/or proposition but comes in shades of grey. It has also been claimed not only by the Inuit but by the federal government that increased self-determination for the Inuit should be viewed not as a reduction of Canadian sovereignty but as a contribution to it. The government, for instance, promoted the creation of Nunavut on the grounds that it would strengthen Arctic sovereignty. Barry Zellen argues that the political outcomes emerging in the Canadian Arctic retain the 'spirit of independence' within 'sovereign duality', where 'the modern state is no longer an opponent, but a powerful partner'. A particularly interesting example of this approach is the role in the north of the Canadian Rangers, a component of the Reserves (and thus of the Canadian Forces) that operates in the north of the country and is composed, in the Arctic, primarily of Inuit.[16] Ranger units are organized along unusual lines from a military point of view (corporals and sergeants are elected by their squads), and the units are designed both to mobilize and to pass on Inuit knowledge. These units, which include among their responsibilities the carrying out of 'sovereignty patrols' (SOVPATs), are far and away the most prominent presence of the Canadian Forces in the Arctic, and both the Canadian government and the Inuit have emphasized the role they play in contributing to Canadian sovereignty there.

Conclusion

This chapter has considered the very large areas of the world's land in which states are far from holding effective authority. It has examined the efforts of states to exert authority in two regions – the lands of the North-West Frontier and the Northwest Passage – said to be central to early twenty-first-century geopolitics. Some similarities can be identified between the cases. Both amply demonstrate the ambiguous and contradictory attitudes that state officials commonly hold towards frontier areas, attitudes which combine the desire to know and control what goes on and a recognition of the economic costs and political risks of doing so. Both are also areas where transnational relationships around land are very visible. The Inuit have mobilized transnationally in pursuit of goals including land claims and regulatory power, and have engaged with transnational corporations operating in the Arctic both as opponents and as partners. The Pashtuns who live in FATA borderlands have long pursued their livelihoods without too much thought for where the Durand Line is, and since the 1970s the region has seen intense transnational flows of people (including *mujahideen*, insurgents and refugees), ideas, weapons and money. The United States has also been a very important actor in both areas.

What stands out more, however, are the differences. Most obviously, FATA is embroiled in an insurgency/civil war. The state's relationship with FATA's residents is still notionally governed by fundamentally colonial institutional structures that have come under increasing criticism in Pakistan and elsewhere, but even those structures are defunct across much of the area. There is a very real sense in which Pakistan is at war with FATA, and the inability (or perhaps unwillingness) of the Pakistani state to control the behaviour of the people there is a huge problem for the country's diplomatic relations. In Canada, on the other hand, there has been relatively little state concern in recent decades that the Inuit themselves need to be brought under control. The concerns constantly stressed by the federal government arise not from the Inuit but from the vastness, the sparse population and inaccessibility of the land, and the worry that 'unused' territory may be susceptible to the (often vaguely specified) sovereign claims of other states. The government's relationship with the Inuit, while certainly filled with tension, conflicting priorities and substantial residues of colonialism, is also in key respects quite hopeful and creative. The Inuit have been able to achieve not just title to land and a role in some types of land regulation but also formal institutions of self-government. A comparison of FATA and the Canadian Arctic gives some sense of the wide range of ways in which frontier people and states engage with one another.

Chapters 2 and 3 have been structured by the distinction between the 'external' and 'internal' territorial relations of states envisioned by political maps of the world. They have also shown, however, that the politics of territory are not so simple. Whether or not the territories of the Pashtuns and the British Columbia first nations discussed in chapter 2 are 'inside' their respective states depends very much on who you ask. The Inuit see themselves as Canadians, but wish to exercise self-determination over the land that they see as their territory. Territorial relations reveal more of a continuum than the 'inside–outside' distinction suggests. This, in combination with the sheer difficulty that states continue to face in trying to exercise control at the frontier, means that state territorial sovereignty is something that will never be 'completed' in practice – whatever the maps may show.

CHAPTER FOUR

Land Booms

What do you think of when you think of Brazil? For most people outside the country, the first images to spring to mind would likely be of the Amazon rainforest and Rio de Janeiro. Fewer would think of the *cerrado*, a massive area of highly biodiverse grassland south and east of the Amazon that covers about a quarter of Brazil's land. Since the 1980s, the conversion of vast amounts of the *cerrado* to capital-intensive industrial farms growing genetically modified crops like soy, corn, cotton and coffee has turned Brazil into a food export superpower. Farms routinely cover tens if not hundreds of thousands of hectares of land. The *cerrado* is one of the great frontiers of our time. At the beginning of the boom, the state's presence in the area was minimal, and the expansion of agriculture often continues to run far ahead of the rule of law. The region is also at the forefront of one of the core dynamics of early twenty-first-century global political economy: rapidly rising demand for land from local and foreign corporations across a wide (but uneven) swath of the South. To some, the conquest of the *cerrado* by agribusiness holds out the hope of feeding the world without deforestation. To others, it is part of a 'global land grab' in which rapacious states and corporations are seizing land at the expense of indigenous people, small farmers, pastoralists, fishers and the environment.[1]

The *cerrado*'s status as a frontier and as an area of rapidly expanding large-scale land acquisition make the region a point of connection between the themes of the preceding chapter and those of the next two. Chapters 4 and 5 examine the transnational role in efforts to transform land regulation and the control of land as property in the global South. This chapter focuses on the role of transnational actors in attempts to make land in the global South available for the agricultural, industrial, residential, commercial, resource extraction, recreation/tourism and infrastructural projects of corporations. The most obviously transnational side of this process, the purchase or lease of land in other countries by TNCs, involves property. Large-scale foreign land acquisitions in the South have surged since the beginning of the global land grab (I dispense with the scare quotes around 'land grab' from here). So, too, has the acquisition of land by corporations in their own countries – often much more important to the land grab than foreign acquisitions are – for the purposes of taking part in transnational production networks.

While large-scale land acquisition is most obviously a question of property (which is inherent to the very concepts of 'acquisition' or 'grab'), corporate land acquisition is deeply influenced by regulation. This chapter also examines the role of transnational actors, including foreign governments, aid agencies, international financial institutions, NGOs and consultants, in shaping the way states in the global South make land available to corporations and in funding what may seem to be largely domestically oriented developments. More diffusely, transnational discourses and visions influence the goals and methods of domestic actors. People in Kuala Lumpur may dream of their city becoming the next Silicon Valley; people in Mexico may seek to follow the South Korean or Chinese path to export stardom; people in Ukraine may imagine transforming their country's 'unproductive' and 'under-utilized' farmland into something resembling the American midwest (or the *cerrado*). This chapter highlights the complex networks of actors, policies and discourses that help and hinder corporate land acquisition, networks in which the transnational and the domestic can be difficult to disentangle.

The projects described below are motivated in large part by the quest for personal and corporate profit. They also often result in the dispossession, perhaps by force and without compensation, of the people who had previously occupied the land. There is more going on here, however, than companies and officials trying to make as much money as possible and not much caring who gets hurt along the way. Another powerful motivation that links these projects (and those discussed in chapter 5) is what Tania Murray Li calls 'the will to improve'. This, simply put, is the desire (sometimes felt as a powerful obligation) to intervene in other people's lives to make them better, and the belief that one knows how to do so effectively. It is the will to, among other things, create prosperity and development, make land use more rational and efficient, reduce conflict, recognize rights and conserve the environment. Arguments about land regulation and property rights often refer to what needs to be done to make a country 'modern' or 'globally competitive' or 'sustainable', and to ensure compliance with putative global 'best practices'. The following chapters contain ample expressions of the will to improve by representatives of domestic and foreign governments, aid agencies, international institutions, corporations, and non-governmental organizations. While the goals in question vary (and often contradict one another), the expressed desire to make life better for others is usually present.

This chapter, then, deals with the interlinked roles of regulation and property in corporate land acquisition – though land's territorial associations also frequently come into play. The next section of the chapter outlines some of the key issues that shape land investment in general, with emphasis on the transnational side. It first examines some of the general reasons that TNCs seek to acquire land abroad by introducing the concepts of foreign direct investment (FDI) and of transnational production networks. It then surveys the challenges domestic firms and especially TNCs face in gaining access to land for investment in the South, and some of the ways they, and southern states, overcome those challenges. The chapter then takes up two of today's most important transnational land investment dynamics. I first introduce the land grabs that seek to establish large-scale corporate agricultural production, with a focus on sub-Saharan Africa. I then examine land booms in the enormous 'peri-urban' areas that surround many cities in the South. India is the example given, though similar dynamics in China will be discussed in chapter 6. Chapter 5 will show that the actors, policies and discourses that characterize transnational land investment can be surprisingly similar to those at work in land titling and environmental conservation.

Transnational land acquisition: motivations, challenges and assistance

Motivations
The acquisition of land by private actors across international borders is far from new. As discussed in chapter 3, the colonial era saw massive movements of Europeans to take up small-scale farming in, especially, the Americas. British imperialism was marked almost from its inception by the idea that taking over land in the colonies for productive purposes was an act of 'improvement' (the original meaning of which was 'to make profitable') that would benefit not just those acquiring the land but all humankind. British enclosures of land as private property were justified by the argument that natives were not making efficient, 'improving' use of the land and were thus wasting nature's bounty (see also chapter 5). Large-scale private cross-border land investments by Europeans and,

later, Americans and Japanese from the mid-nineteenth century to the 1970s were dominated by plantation agriculture, ranching and resource extraction. The search for cheap land and cheap labour subject to light, if any, regulation drove these investments, and their importance has surged with the recent global land grab.

The dominant types of investments (in terms of the amount of capital invested if not necessarily of the amount of land acquired), however, have changed since the 1970s. One of the ways late twentieth and early twenty-first-century economic globalization has been most novel is the creation of transnational production networks. Rapid developments in communications and transportation technology, combined with the liberalization of global trade and investment flows and intensifying corporate competition, have pushed TNCs to distribute the production of the different components that make up their products between factories in different countries. The goal is to maximize profits by locating design, manufacturing and assembly in countries where workers with the required skills can be hired most cheaply and where land with access to transportation and infrastructure can be acquired for the least money. The establishment of production networks organized regionally or even globally has relocated a substantial amount of manufacturing capacity to the South. Such networks are also increasingly common in the agricultural and fisheries sectors. And all the nodes in these networks – the car parts factories, the computer assembly plants, the avocado fields and chicken-processing facilities, the warehouses and shipping centres – need land.

Transnational production networks have been set up in good part through foreign direct investment.[2] FDI takes place when a company acquires a substantial and lasting interest in an enterprise in a country other than the one in which it is based. The two major forms are 'greenfield' investments, in which the TNC establishes a new wholly or partially owned subsidiary overseas, and mergers and acquisitions, in which TNCs invest in an already existing company abroad. FDI plays a major role in all sectors of the world economy, including manufacturing, services, resource extraction, agriculture, retail and transportation. While FDI flows in 2010 were well below the levels reached before the global financial crisis, the world figure of US$1.24 trillion still represents a staggering amount of money. Until the mid-2000s, inflows of FDI went primarily to the developed world, but, since the crisis began, the share of the countries that the UN Conference on Trade and Development (UNCTAD) calls 'developing' and 'transition' economies has spiked. In 2010, inflows to these economies exceeded 50 per cent of global FDI for the first time. Some countries in the South receive huge amounts of FDI; others get hardly any. Southern countries are also increasingly prominent sources of outward FDI, much of which goes to other parts of the South. The top five economies in terms of inflows in 2010 were the US, China, Hong Kong, Belgium and Brazil, while spots 1–5 on the outflows list were held by the US, Germany, France, Hong Kong and China.

While FDI has reshaped the global political economy, the impact of transnational production networks goes far beyond FDI. TNCs sometimes source products by buying or establishing foreign subsidiaries, but they also do so through 'contract manufacturing, services outsourcing, contract farming, franchising, licensing, management contracts, and other types of contractual relationship through which TNCs coordinate the activities of host country firms, without owning a stake in those firms'. UNCTAD estimates that TNC-linked production under these non-ownership-based firm-to-firm connections generated at least US$2 trillion in sales in 2010, with contract manufacturing and services making up as much as US$1.3 trillion of that figure. The crucial implication is that analyses of the transnational side of land investments will underestimate its significance if they only examine FDI. Companies looking for land on which to set up operations in their home country – Thai companies canning tuna in Thailand, Mexican companies in Mexican *maquilladoras* – often do so to undertake contract production or outsourced work as part of a TNC's production network.

Challenges

The land requirements of different types of investment vary dramatically. A TNC setting up an oil palm plantation will want tens of thousands of hectares. A high-tech manufacturing firm or seafood processing plant may need just a few hectares with reliable electricity supply in reasonable proximity to an airport. Almost all investments, though, need *some* access to land. Companies, however, frequently find that they cannot simply buy or lease the land they need on the private market, for two main reasons. One is the regulations that surround land conversion, ownership, rental and use, regulations which can be particularly restrictive for foreigners and foreign companies. The other is the practical difficulty of assembling large parcels of land in the parts of the South where TNCs generally want to undertake manufacturing or agricultural investments. For both reasons, states play a vital role in making land available to domestic and foreign corporations.

Regulations powerfully shape the market for land. Among the most important are the zoning regulations that state what different land areas may be used for and what uses are forbidden. Industrial use, for instance, is often restricted to areas specifically zoned for that purpose. Getting land converted from one zoning category to another can be a time-consuming and difficult process. This is especially the case for land zoned as agricultural, which is often, in the peri-urban areas around major cities in both the North and the South, the primary type of land that developers wish to convert to more profitable industrial, commercial, residential or leisure uses. Acquiring and using land can also be complicated by the overlapping, opaque, byzantine and fitfully implemented systems of land titling, regulation and administration that characterize much of the South, a topic explored further in chapter 5. Finally, in some countries all land is formally owned by the state, and in others large amounts are; would-be acquirers have to deal with the government to get access to this land.

Regulatory restrictions on land sales and leases generally increase when foreigners are involved. Few international markets are as illiberal as the market for land (one of them is the market for labour), which is not subject to any over-arching regulatory agreement or institution such as those of the World Trade Organization. Most countries distinguish between citizens and foreigners when it comes to land owner-ship, and most have regulations designed to restrict foreign control over land. A few go so far as to ban foreign land own-ership outright. The range of approaches is enormous, and I can only sketch some of the main parameters. There are three major motivations behind state efforts to control foreign land purchases and leases. One is national security. Countries including Greece, Italy, Mexico and Spain restrict foreign land acquisition in border areas. A second is concern over for-eign domination of the national economy. States restrict land ownership for purposes including limiting FDI and keeping control of food production in domestic hands. A third is indi-rect control over immigration. Moving to a country becomes more difficult if foreigners face land ownership restrictions.

What exactly is regulated, and the types of regulation used, also vary substantially from country to country. On the former question, restrictions on foreign ownership are commonly based on the type of land use or zoning (agricultural land, again, is often controlled), on the land's location (rural, urban, close to the border) and on the total amount of the country's land held by foreigners or by any particular foreign individual or company. Types of regulation include constitutional bans on foreign land ownership, rules forcing foreigners to partner with local companies to buy or lease land, differential taxation of land transfers to foreigners, and tighter requirements for prior approval or reporting of such transfers. The effectiveness of all of these regulations in any given country, finally, is an open question. Regulations may contain large loopholes, foreigners often find ways to comply with the letter of the law while violating its spirit, and sometimes straightforward bribery can make obstacles vanish.

Perhaps the most compelling general explanation for the complex webs of regulation that govern land use and ownership by citizens and foreigners alike is that of Karl Polanyi.[3] Polanyi argued in *The Great Transformation* that while land, labour and money may be available for sale on the market, they are in fact 'fictitious commodities' because they were not originally created to be sold for profit. Land existed before the market (indeed, before humans), and it provides indispensable social and natural services. Polanyi claimed that allowing the fate of land to be determined solely by market forces would lead to its degradation and to the destruction of the agriculture and nature on which humans depend. For this reason, people and governments inevitably try to protect land from the free market. Certainly the facts that a laissez-faire market for land exists almost nowhere in the world and that governments regulate land sales and use for a wide range of purposes suggest that few, if any, societies are prepared to tolerate a genuinely liberal land market.

Regulatory issues like overlapping or unclear tenure regimes, restrictions on land sales and conversion, and controls on foreign land purchases and leases thus complicate corporate land acquisition, and often mean that companies seeking land will need the state's assistance or even partnership. The other main reason states play a central role in the land market in the South is the simple practical difficulty of assembling substantial parcels of land. Much of the land targeted in contemporary booms is relatively high-quality agricultural land. For large-scale agricultural investments, this is because companies tend to want land that is good for farming. Industrial, commercial, residential and tourist/leisure projects, on the other hand, usually do best in peri-urban areas close to transportation networks, infrastructure and urban demand, and, since cities tend to be located in good agricultural areas, building such projects likely means converting farmland. Large-scale land investments in the South thus very often require engagement with hundreds if not thousands of small-scale farming households. Straightforward purchases on the market are unlikely to make much headway under such conditions, given farmer unwillingness to sell, the likelihood of hold-outs waiting for a better price and worries about potential litigation deriving from unclear title (if the current holders are even recognized as having a right to the land). Michael Levien quotes an Indian official: 'If they have to talk to farmers, it will be a problem for industrial people to procure the land. If you go and ask the farmer, can it happen? No! They will come and cut your head [off]!'[4]

Assistance

Regulatory and practical obstacles mean that making land available to corporations can be a challenge for state agencies. It is also, however, a project they are often keen to undertake. Investment in land can contribute to the fulfilment of a wide range of state priorities that mostly fall under the heading of the will to improve. As chapter 3 demonstrated, investments at the frontier can buttress claims to sovereignty over territory.

Foreign and domestic investment in agricultural, industrial, commercial, residential and tourist projects and in the infrastructure they require is widely seen as promoting development and economic growth by shifting land from less to more productive uses. When land previously devoted to small-scale family farms is converted to large-scale, well-capitalized agriculture, industrial parks, shopping malls or high-end apartment complexes, the value of the economic activity that takes place on the land can skyrocket, and tax receipts will skyrocket along with it. More specific goals may include attracting FDI and promoting exports. Making land available is often seen to be fundamental to a country's (or a state/province's, or a city's) competitiveness in the global economy.

State officials also pursue land investments for more sordid reasons. When land is taken over, its former holders rarely receive more than a fraction of the land's new value. Payments for such land on the market, or compensation paid by the state when land is expropriated, are generally low. In many cases, officials refuse to accept that the occupants have any claim to compensation and pay them nothing at all. Even in best-case scenarios, the gap between the price paid for the land and its new value under more 'productive' use can be very large. This gap creates massive financial opportunities for the people in charge of conversion. When the government or the private purchaser sells or rents the land to other users at near-market price, there will be a windfall profit on the transaction. When state officials provide the land to corporations for little or no payment (as often happens), the windfall accrues to the company. In either case, the opportunities for state officials to enrich themselves through kickbacks and payments for regulatory approvals are enormous. Even when they do not receive direct financial benefits, officials may be able to reward allies and supporters with cheap but valuable land. Large-scale land investments can thus look doubly appealing to the politicians and bureaucrats with the power to approve them: good for the economy and good for them personally.

Given all these potential positives, state officials try to help investors in land to get around their regulatory and practical challenges. One common approach is the creation of special economic zones, 'spaces of exception', for investment where land is made available and much of the national regulatory framework is suspended. The appeal of such zones is easy to see if the Polanyian argument above is correct; they create a spatially delimited area where companies are free to do as they like without dismantling the whole framework of protective regulation around land. In many countries, however, some of the special incentives previously offered to companies only in the zones are now available across the national territory. Incentives can range from free land to exemption from taxation and labour regulations to guaranteed access to water. Many countries (and sub-national jurisdictions) in the South now have investment promotion agencies that aggressively seek out foreign investment. Indeed, many governments find themselves in a 'race to the bottom' in which they desperately try to outbid each other by offering ever more enticing deal-sweeteners to foreign firms. With respect to the practicalities of making land available, the task of assembling a single large parcel of land out of a large number of tiny ones is often performed in part by land brokers, private figures or local politicians who employ cash, promises, information, social networks, political power and sometimes force to convince people to let go of their land. While this can be enough, more often the state needs to get involved. Legal and regulatory frameworks, appeals to public purpose and national development goals and, at the limit, the police or the army thus take over where the market fails.

Rich country governments and IFIs also give direct and indirect assistance to TNCs and other private actors looking for land in the South. Direct assistance includes investment in the firms and the provision of risk insurance against potential problems like expropriation, breach of contract and civil war. Indirect assistance includes the many ways donor governments and IFIs encourage and pressure states in the South to open themselves up to foreign investment in general and investment in land in particular. The United States, for instance, makes developing country eligibility for the benefits of its Millennium Challenge Account (MCA) and African Growth and Opportunity Act conditional on the implementation of free market reforms, including investment liberalization. MCA funds, according to the Millennium Challenge Corporation, are to be limited to countries that ensure that 'state intervention in the goods and land market is generally limited to regulation and/or legislation to smooth out market imperfections.' The various arms of the World Bank Group also work to get states in the South to open up to investment, including in land. Their methods include policy advice on liberalizing investment and land access policies, technical assistance in the actual drafting of laws and regulations, maintaining indicators that let investors compare countries' investment-friendliness, and help (including policy advice and direct funding) for states creating or expanding investment promotion agencies.[5] Finally, bilateral investment treaties between governments restrict the ability of states to limit foreign investment. All of this assistance (and arm-twisting) has contributed substantially to the liberalization of rules around foreign land investment in many countries since the 1990s and can be understood in terms of the project of opening up the world to capitalist investment discussed in chapter 2. The momentum, however, is not all in one direction. Countries including Argentina, Bolivia, Brazil and Ecuador have recently moved to restrict foreign investment in land.

The agricultural land grab

In October 2008, the international non-governmental organization GRAIN published a briefing paper entitled 'Seized! The 2008 Land Grab for Food and Financial Security'. The report was the first overview of the sudden increase in large-scale, cross-border land acquisitions in the global South that began around 2007. Some of the land acquisition projects brought to light in GRAIN's work and in the subsequent explosion of research and reporting on the global land grab have been nothing short of astonishing. Saudi Arabia's Binladin Group, for instance, aims to grow 7 million tons of rice per year on 700,000 hectares of land in six West African countries through its AgroGlobe project. Reports suggest that the South Korean company Ho Myoung Farm is raising cattle, sheep and goats on 216,000 hectares of farmland in Australia. El Tejar, a company based in Argentina that is partly owned by a London-based hedge fund, the World Bank's International Finance Corporation and an American private equity fund, is said to be farming 800,000 hectares in Argentina, Brazil and Uruguay.⁶ Some of the most dramatic projects reported in the media have been delayed, scaled back or cancelled since they were announced, and substantial reductions in project scale between the initial announcement, formal land transfers, actual land acquisition and planting, and harvesting have been a common feature of land grab projects. The figures just quoted, however, give a sense of the scale of the ambitions of some would-be transnational investors in agriculture.

Large-scale land purchases and leases across international borders are, again, not new, but the surge since 2007 demands both description and explanation. Both tasks are complicated by the paucity of solid comparative information. The data problems are highlighted by the extent of the variation between existing estimates of the scope of the land grab. While it is clear that at least several tens of millions of hectares have been targeted, different inventories have come up with figures of 46.6 million, 60 million, 80 million and 225 million hectares.[7] There is more agreement on the major investing countries, which include China, the Gulf States, Libya, Egypt, Russia, the US and the UK; investments have mostly been in sub-Saharan Africa, Eastern Europe, Central Asia, Latin America and South-East Asia, though that list does not narrow things down much. Large-scale international land acquisitions have taken place in pursuit of many goals, including agriculture, mining, oil and gas exploration, industry, tourism, residential developments, speculation on rising land prices and even conservation (see chapter 5). My analysis focuses on agriculture. The primary goal of agricultural investments is the establishment of intensive, monocropped production of fuel, food and fibre crops like oil palm, jatropha, rice, soybeans, sugar cane, wheat, maize and fast-growing trees like eucalyptus and acacia.

The main actors interacting around large-scale transnational land acquisitions can be divided into four categories. On the investor side, the central players have been governments, notably those in Middle Eastern and East Asian countries; transnational corporations; and financial market players like private equity groups. On the recipient side, second, governments and state agencies play the key role, as they have regulatory control over investment and often claim the land which investors are interested in as state property. Domestic capital can also be important through the joint ventures, subcontracting agreements and other tie-ups it forms with international investors. (While it is important to note that, in most countries, domestic capital plays a more central direct role than does foreign capital in the expansion of large-scale agriculture, and the land grab is thus not an entirely or even a primarily foreign affair, domestic and transnational capital are also often deeply interconnected.) Village and community groups (or at least elites) can also be involved in negotiations over the use of their land, though they are often excluded. Third, as noted in the previous section, international financial institutions (notably the World Bank Group), regional development banks, aid agencies and consultants have promoted transnational land acquisition by providing direct financing and insurance against risks, giving policy advice and encouraging recipient governments to liberalize their regulations around land. Finally, groups trying to resist or at least regulate the land grab have included landholders in the affected areas, NGOs, social movements, academics, journalists, and international institutions like the World Bank (again) and other groups from within the UN system, such as the Food and Agriculture Organization's Committee on World Food Security.

The key trigger for the agricultural land grab was the massive spike in commodity prices that took place in 2007–8. Between January and May 2008 alone, the price of rice rose by 191%, of maize by 43%, of soybeans by 48% and of petroleum by 66%.[8] As the price of agricultural commodities went through the roof, it encouraged acquisitions of arable land both because agriculture looked increasingly profitable and because the land itself was an increasingly attractive investment. The latter motivation was especially compelling for financial sector actors fleeing from the meltdown of the more baroque components of the global financial system and looking for places to put their money. Rising oil prices, meanwhile, had a complex set of influences on farming: they discouraged agricultural production by making inputs and transportation more expensive, but encouraged it by raising demand for crops like oil palm, maize and sugar cane that could be used to produce biofuels to substitute for expensive petroleum. High biofuel crop prices were also supported by government policies, notably in the European Union and the US, that promoted or mandated for ostensibly environmental purposes the replacement of petroleum consumption with fuels derived from plants. While commodity prices dropped off abruptly in 2008–9, they have since risen again, and the sense that the world has entered an extended period of high commodity prices has stimulated interest in investment in agricultural production.

For agribusiness companies and financial sector actors, the main motivations for land grabs are profit through production and speculation in the value of crops and land. Many governments, however, have become intensely nervous not just about rising food and fuel prices but also, in the wake of temporary bans on the export of commodities like rice and wheat by major suppliers, about the prospect that their access may be cut off. Middle Eastern states highly dependent on food imports and East Asian ones reliant on imported food and fuel have thus begun not only to support but directly to engage in overseas land acquisitions to try to guarantee supplies. Land grabs here thus have a geopolitical, as well as a profit-oriented, motivation. While it is not clear what percentage of production from land-grab projects is exported and what percentage of that goes to the investing country, it *is* clear that international land investment derives not only from the desire to make profits on international commodity markets but also from a push to *avoid* such markets by securing supplies for the home state even in cases of market instability and export cut-offs. The investment drive created by the intersection of all these developments, finally, met with a much more receptive response in the South than it would have, say, two decades earlier. As discussed above, many governments in potential recipient states had, by the late 2000s, liberalized their land regulations and introduced new incentive schemes (including offering land more or less for free) in an effort to attract FDI. States including Cambodia, Ethiopia, Mozambique, the Philippines and Tanzania now actively seek land investment.

Proponents of large-scale land acquisitions for agriculture do not just argue in terms of profits and secure food supplies for the people of East Asia and the Middle East. They also argue that they hold out the promise of substantial benefits for local people and the environment. The supportive policy discourse begins by pointing out that a very large amount of arable land in the South is 'under-utilized' (not as productively farmed as it could be) or 'unused'. The poverty of the huge numbers of people who farm 'under-utilized' land, it is argued, is both a result and a cause of the 'yield gap' between current yields per hectare and those that could be achieved if the best existing practices were used. Large-scale international (and domestic) agricultural investments hold out the promise of ameliorating this situation by bringing together corporate capital, technology, managerial know-how, infrastructure (including irrigation) and distribution networks with the under-capitalized agricultural land and labour of the South. The World Bank's 2010 report *Rising Global Interest in Farmland: Can it Yield Sustainable and Equitable Benefits?* quantifies the potential benefits by locating countries in the South on a grid that shows their 'yield gap' and their 'ratio of non-forested, noncultivated area suitable for rain-fed production relative to what is actually cultivated'.

Those who make the case for the positive side of large-scale land investment usually recognize that these projects can go horribly wrong, and they do not sign off on just any kind of investment. They may, for instance, seek to prioritize models in which farmers retain their own land and grow under contract to and with the assistance of corporations (contract farming) over projects based on plantation agriculture in which workers are low-paid, usually landless employees. They also emphasize (in an argument discussed in detail in chapter 5) that when land *is* acquired, it should be purchased from its current holders under fair conditions.

Klaus Deininger argues that 'If rights are well defined, if land markets are not monopolized, and if information is accessible to all, voluntary transactions where land is valued at market prices should ensure that a mutually satisfying outcome is achieved.' They highlight, too, the importance of governance frameworks. One international land investment governance initiative is the set of voluntary Principles for Responsible Agricultural Investment (RAI) developed by the World Bank, the Food and Agricultural Organization (FAO), UNCTAD and the International Fund for Agricultural Development (IFAD). These principles are meant to ensure, among other things, social and environmental sustainability, the protection of existing property and resource rights and consultation with the affected people.[9]

Support for the land grab, then, derives in substantial part from the will to improve. The claim is that large-scale investments in land and agriculture in the South, when done right, benefit not just investors but host governments, landholders and communities, and can contribute, ultimately, to the goal of feeding the world. It is not just transnational policy intellectuals who see things this way. One of the most striking aspects of Fred Pearce's 2012 book *The Land Grabbers* is the consistency with which the many corporate land investors he interviews affirm that their projects are good for the world, for the hungry and poor, for the environment and even for the people the investments are displacing.

Opponents of the land grab tell a very different story: one of dispossession and environmental degradation. They criticize, first, the notion of 'unused' arable land, which, they argue, does not exist. There is virtually no arable land in the South that is not being used by somebody for something. Often, land that the state claims is 'unused' or 'vacant' when negotiating with investors is in fact full of farmers. Saturnino M. Borras Jr and Jennifer Franco report visiting an enormous tract of land in the Philippines that had been allocated for large-scale investment and that was classified as 'uninhabited', but that was in fact 'significantly populated' and under productive agricultural use.[10] Even when land is not currently being farmed, it is usually being used for something – fallow for swidden agriculture, grazing land for cattle, a source of wood and other forest products. Large-scale land acquisitions virtually always take place on land that is occupied and used. For critics, the global land grab essentially amounts to the seizure of land from small-scale farmers, fishers and pastoralists in the South who do not have the secure property rights or the political power to resist this push. The World Bank's finding that intended land investment is negatively correlated with recognition for rural land rights in the recipient country supports the argument that investors want land that can be grabbed without too much difficulty.

Critics highlight a wide range of other problems beyond dispossession. They are concerned about the very limited job-creation prospects of large-scale, plantation-style agriculture (one foreign-owned farm in the *cerrado* has 40,000 hectares of land and 180 workers). They point out that governments in the South are giving investors essentially permanent control (through sale or very long-term leases) of enormous amounts of land in return for minimal payments or, often, for literally nothing. They worry about the prospect of foreign schemes exporting large amounts of food from food-insecure countries; about competition for water between foreign schemes and local farmers, especially where governments have promised water supplies to investors; and about the social and environmental damage done by large-scale land investment. With respect to governance, they see the voluntary principles of the RAI as inadequate (at best) under the conditions of near-secrecy and of enormous asymmetries of power and information that characterize so many land investment deals.

They note, too, that even well-intentioned and capable govern-ments will struggle to deal with all of these problems when they are competing for investment with other countries that may not be so fastidious, and when they are parties to invest-ment treaties that restrict their ability to impose controls. Another constant refrain in *The Land Grabbers* is how badly land deals often turn out for the people on the receiving end.

Land grabs and customary land rights in sub-Saharan Africa
The global land grab is a multifaceted phenomenon, and it is not possible here to cover all its aspects in detail. One very important issue that provides a point of connection to chapter 5, however, is the role of regulation and law in shaping what land ends up getting taken over for large-scale land acquisi-tions. What is the regulatory framework within which people find that they can no longer hold onto land that they claim as their property (and, perhaps, their territory)? I take this question up by means of a brief comparative survey of condi-tions in sub-Saharan Africa. This region has been identified by the World Bank as particularly 'land-abundant' (though individual countries like Rwanda and Malawi may have little uncultivated arable land) and as an area where the 'yield gap' is especially wide. Sub-Saharan Africa is also, according to most reports, the main region targeted in the global land grab. The World Bank found that 23 per cent of all global 'putative demand' for large-scale land acquisition is accounted for by just five African countries: Sudan, Ethiopia, Nigeria, Ghana and Mozambique. Using a different calculation method that is based on inventory data and includes domestic acquisition, the Bank found that the period 2004–2008 had seen 4 million hectares of large-scale land acquisitions in Sudan, 2.7 million in Mozambique, 1.6 million in Liberia (including renewals of existing projects), and 1.2 million in Ethiopia.[11]

While the countries of sub-Saharan Africa are extremely

diverse, large-scale land acquisitions are shaped by some common regional land acquisition trends. One is the finding that the majority of land acquisitions are of public rather than private land. This is because the state is the ultimate legal owner of most or all of the land in most sub-Saharan African countries, and investors thus generally need to acquire land directly from the government. There has also been a strong recent tendency in the region towards the liberalization and facilitation of foreign land acquisition, with many states becoming active promoters. Common moves have included the creation of investment promotion agencies that seek to streamline FDI in land and the state creation of 'land banks' (for instance, in Ghana, Tanzania and Zambia) for foreign investment projects. Sub-Saharan African governments have, for the most part, fully accepted the arguments about the development benefits of FDI promoted in the region by the World Bank and other IFIs.

While the state claims formal ownership of land in most countries in sub-Saharan Africa, rural land use and rights are very often governed in practice by customary tenure regimes at the village, tribal or clan level. The extent to which customary land tenure is formally recognized by the state varies greatly by country. Liz Alden Wily divides the national land laws of 30 sub-Saharan African states into three categories on the basis of their treatment of customary land tenure. In the first group of six states (Ghana, Mozambique, South Africa, South Sudan, Tanzania and Uganda),

> new national laws make customary land tenure a fully legal and equivalent route through which land rights may be owned and transacted, and explicitly inclusive of properties which communities own and use in common. Just as importantly, even when these rights have not been entrenched in formal certificates of title, this legal support is by law bound to be upheld.[12]

In a second group of ten states, there is some recognition of customary tenure, but it is substantially less robust than in the first group. In the remaining states, customary landholders are highly vulnerable to dispossession, as they 'are considered to have no more than permissive occupancy and use rights on national or government lands'.

Greater recognition for customary land rights seems like a positive development from the point of view of allowing land-holders to resist land grabs. Two points, however, suggest a more ambivalent conclusion. One is that, while consultation with customary landholders may be an important part of state land allocation to investors in some countries, there is quite consistent evidence demonstrating that consultations are generally carried out quickly, under pressure and in conditions of unequal access to information (including information about the process itself) and to political and economic power. Local elites often ride roughshod over community preferences and strike deals that benefit themselves. Rights alone, then, are not enough.

Second, in countries with more robust systems of customary rights, communities or their leaders are often direct participants in negotiations with investors over land reallocation. A striking aspect of land governance in some countries since the 1990s has been a simultaneous move towards more openness to foreign land acquisition and stronger recognition for customary land rights. These developments are not contradictory but complementary: one of the reasons for the move towards greater recognition of customary land rights in some countries was the desire to make it *easier* for communities to alienate their land to investors, and thus to support the government push for increased FDI. For investors, clear allocation of property rights to communities can make them appealing negotiating partners. The information provided to potential investors on the website of the Sierra Leone

Investment and Export Promotion Agency, for instance, states that the country's 'communal/chiefdom land tenure system and strong government facilitation makes land easy to obtain in most agricultural areas through secure, long-term leases'.[13] This process whereby formal recognition of customary or indigenous land rights *facilitates* the making of land deals was also, as noted in chapter 3, a result of the settlement of Inuit land claims in the Canadian Arctic.

These findings raise the question of whether formal recognition of customary tenure makes much difference in conditions of unequal political and economic power and intense demand for land. Laura A. German, George Schoneveld and Esther Mwangi conclude their detailed overview of customary rights and large-scale land acquisition in Ghana, Mozambique, Tanzania and Zambia with the bleak observation that, while there are large variations in the legal systems and acquisition processes in the four countries, 'in the vast majority of cases outcomes are similar: customary rights to vast areas of land are lost – often permanently, with limited to no compensation.' The World Bank, on the other hand, argues that customary rights can shape outcomes, noting that 'In Tanzania, where land rights are firmly vested with villages, less than 50,000 ha were transferred to investors between January 2004 and June 2009. By contrast, over the same period in Mozambique, 2.7 million were transferred.'[14]

Land booms on the urban fringe

India's average annual growth in gross national income, already a healthy 5.2 per cent between 1990 and 2002, accelerated to a positively East Asian 8.4 per cent in the period 2003–2010. As the urban economy boomed, demand for land in reasonable proximity to urban areas took off. One way the central government tried to meet this demand was through a new policy framework for special economic zones (SEZs) launched in 2005 and analysed by Michael Levien in two recent articles.[15] Under this framework, state governments acquire parcels of land from the people (generally farmers) holding them. The states make this land available to private developers who prepare it for business use and lease it to other companies wishing to use it for industrial, information technology (IT) or other productive purposes. The latter companies receive not only the land but a range of other incentives, including tax exemptions and a streamlined regulatory process. SEZ developers are also allowed to use up to 50 per cent of the land for purposes other than export-oriented business parks. The real-estate developments and shopping/leisure complexes that they tend to put up on this land are often more profitable than the industrial part of the project. These opportunities make peri-urban zones particularly attractive. The model is extremely popular; as of 2011, close to 600 SEZs had been approved. Levien stresses that the strategy has been driven overwhelmingly by domestic actors (public and private), and that both the developers of SEZs and the companies that inhabit them are largely Indian. However, the policy's goals, which include encouraging FDI, promoting exports and increasing foreign exchange earnings, are strongly internationally oriented.

The SEZ strategy has encountered substantial obstacles. Many high-profile projects (including some enormous potential foreign investments) have been stopped or stalled, and few large SEZs have started operation. Much of the problem involves the difficulties, noted above, of assembling large landholdings out of the tiny farms of hundreds if not thousands of households. State governments try to get around these problems by invoking the colonial-era Land Acquisition Act, which allows them to acquire land through eminent domain (the compulsory purchase of land by the state) if it is to be used for 'public purposes' – a concept that could conceivably be stretched to include industrial zones supporting national goals like export promotion, but that does not exactly conjure up visions of shopping malls and golf courses. Compensation is generally determined with reference to the land's prior agricultural value (and may not properly reflect even that), rather than to the much more lucrative uses to which it is about to be put. Farmers thus find themselves being forcefully ejected from their land and paid a pittance (at best) for it. Many have fought back. Indeed, farmers have been so successful in their resistance to the SEZ push, and have created such problems for both domestic and foreign investment in SEZs, that they have called the entire strategy into question and raised the land question as 'perhaps the biggest obstacle to capitalist development in India today'. As a consequence, when Levien writes that 'Indian states are thus competing with each other to be the best expropriators of the peasantry',[16] we need to understand 'best' to mean 'most skilful' rather than (necessarily) 'most brutal'.

Levien's detailed study of Mahindra World City (MWC), an SEZ outside Jaipur and one of the exceptional projects that are actually up and running, emphasizes this last point. This 1,200-plus-hectare site will eventually have five sector-specific zones in addition to a 'Lifestyle Zone' made up of 'elite residential colonies',[17] but as of 2011 only the IT zone – which counts Deutsche Bank and the Indian IT giant Infosys among its tenants – is operational. The Zone is being developed as a joint venture between Mahindra Lifespaces Developers and the public Rajasthan Industrial Development and Investment Corporation, with Mahindra doing the land and infrastructure development. The land on which MWC is being constructed is comprised of 405 hectares of formerly state-owned (but locally used) grazing land and 810 hectares of private farmland acquired by eminent domain. Although the land was forcibly acquired from farmers without consultation, MWC has not been subject to the kinds of contention witnessed at so many other proposed SEZ sites. Levien argues that this is largely because of the form of compensation given to some former landholders, who received 25 per cent of their original land area 'as developed commercial and residential plots adjacent to the project'.[18] This neoliberal strategy of turning potential opponents into property-owning stakeholders worked very well, but not because it benefited everyone; rather, it split opposition by benefiting some villagers, notably the ones who were already relatively well off. Many people, however, have seen their standard of living badly eroded by the loss of their land to MWC, which provides only limited and low-level work to the former inhabitants of the Zone's land. Levien 'did not encounter one person from any of the villages who is directly employed by Mahindra, Infosys or Deutsche Bank'.[19]

Michael Goldman's research on Bangalore takes up a range of similar issues in the context not of a 'second-tier' city like Jaipur, but rather at the heart of 'India Shining'.[20] Goldman focuses on efforts to push forward three enormous and land-intensive projects linked to turning Bangalore into a 'world-city': the Bangalore International Airport (BIA, 28 sq. km), the IT Corridor (113 sq. km) and the Bangalore–Mysore Infrastructure Corridor (BMIC, 117 sq. km). Several themes from the MWC story are also prominent in Bangalore. One is the central role of parastatals (companies controlled in whole or in part by the government) armed with the stick of eminent domain, in this case the Karnataka Industrial Areas Development Board (KIADB), in acquiring huge parcels of land for ostensibly 'public purposes'. Another is the enormous opportunities for windfall profits that derive from land sales and expropriations at risibly low prices. Goldman argues that the sums at stake are so substantial that the 'management of this land acquisition process has become the main source of revenue and wealth accumulation in Bangalore today, and the main political tussle amongst the political parties and the parastatal agencies'. Third, the most profitable parts of some projects are, again, the opportunities to create combined residential/shopping/leisure developments. The BIA and the BMIC are framed as infrastructural projects built around an airport and a motorway respectively, but both are attractive to investors primarily because of the opportunities they present for real-estate development.

Goldman's 'speculative urbanism' in Bangalore is much more transnational than Levien's account of India's SEZs. Three points stand out. First, the models, assumptions and frameworks that make up the national vision of IT-driven industrialization and urbanization are deeply embedded in transnational policy networks. India's 'liberalization through urbanization' agenda is, Goldman argues, 'cultivated, sponsored and legitimated by transnational policy networks comprising officials/consultants from the World Bank, Asian Development Bank, Pricewaterhouse Coopers, chambers of commerce, and elite international urban planning programs and fora'. At the city level, too, networks incorporating not just Indian officials and business elites but also IFI and aid agency staff, non-resident Indians and NGOs with international ties are of central importance in shaping urban governance. Second, international capital (public and private), and the conditions that come attached to it, are strongly in evidence in Bangalore's urban mega-projects. A number of key parastatal agencies (including the KIADB) are substantially financed by, and in some cases were actually established by, IFIs, notably the World Bank and the Asian Development Bank. The central government's own urban investment strategy, too, makes billions of dollars available to cities but imposes conditions that include forming partnerships with foreign companies, borrowing capital from international markets, and following IFI policy agendas. Third, international investors are playing a prominent role in building the new developments and in occupying them. FDI in Indian real estate is expanding extremely quickly, and international investors are involved in building the airport and the BMIC. In a passage that resonates with similar developments in other countries, notably the Philippines, Goldman states that 'new townships being built outside Bangalore are being owned, developed and governed by real estate and construction firms from other world cities.'

Trying to pull apart the 'Indian' and the 'transnational' elements of Bangalore's urban mega-projects would not be a rewarding endeavour. It is more important to emphasize Goldman's claim that 'Land speculation and active dispossession inside and surrounding the city of Bangalore is the main business of its government today.' The land areas involved are staggering: the IT Corridor alone is meant to be one and a half times the size of Paris, while the BMIC envisions strips of developments on 8,500 hectares of land along a 130-km motorway connecting Mysore and Bangalore. That land is not empty. Goldman notes that more than 200,000 people will be displaced by the BMIC alone. There is resistance, but it faces both networks of political-economic power and regulatory frameworks (some inherited from the colonial period) that make the challenge an imposing one.

Conclusion

This chapter has explored the complex and powerful transnational dynamics involved in large-scale corporate land acquisition in the South. This role is most obvious when transnational corporations buy or lease land across international borders, a process at the heart of the 'global land grab'. But it goes far beyond that to include the way southern companies acquire land in order to participate in transnational production networks, the efforts of IFIs and northern governments to influence land and investment rules, the policy discourses and visions that inspire across borders, and the transnational networks of NGOs and organizations that seek to oppose or to govern the land grab. Similarly, while corporate investment in land might seem to be primarily a question of property (as implied by the pejorative term 'grab' and the more neutral 'acquisition'), it is also profoundly influenced by the regulations that seek to determine the conditions under which land can be held. Land regulations almost everywhere still recognize that land cannot be fully exposed to market forces – that its commodity status is at some level 'fictitious' – but many of these restrictions are being removed. Regulatory restrictions, too, are not of much use when power trumps law. Dispossession, usually with minimal compensation and often by force, is at the heart of the integration of all of this land into the global corporate economy. When people contest that dispossession, they often do so not just because they see the land as their property and because the rules, as they understand them, are being broken. The territorial connections of identity and belonging that people feel to their land can also be fundamental to the politics of resistance, as chapter 6 will demonstrate.

CHAPTER FIVE

Titling and Conservation

Chapter 4 called attention, in the context of large-scale corporate land acquisitions, to the ways transnational actors and discourses can influence property rights and the regulation of land use in the countries of the South. This chapter explores two processes that may, at least in terms of the numbers of people affected by them over the last two centuries, be the most significant areas of such transnational influence: *titling* and *conservation*.[1] Titling is the process by which the holders of land are given formalized, 'full' state-backed rights to it, including the right of transfer. Conservation projects subject land to regulations designed to protect the environment, most prominently by demarcating it as a protected area or a park. Transnational interventions in both processes shape the ways in which enormous numbers of people in the South can, cannot or must use their land, and even whether they can hold it at all. As in chapter 4, the focus here will be on the transnational side of these issues, but it is important to note that local and national forces are often the main players involved in promoting and responding to projects of titling and conservation.

The two ideas at the heart of this chapter – that rules need to exist to assure people that they will be able to hold on to what's theirs, and that human interaction with what we now call 'nature' needs to be regulated – are fundamental to all societies. The more specific approaches to these questions discussed here, however, primarily trace their ancestry to early modern Britain. The ideas of private property, improvement and the wise and rational use of nature are profoundly linked in the history of British capitalism. They were also fundamental to the form and justification of British imperialism. The 'improving' rationale for British colonial land enclosures was noted in chapter 4. Surveying property boundaries and governing property were also central aspects of British imperialism from an early date, as witnessed by the mid-seventeenth-century Down Survey of Ireland and the 1793 Permanent Settlement discussed in Ranajit Guha's aptly titled classic *A Rule of Property for Bengal*. Close concern with conservation and resource management in the colonies came later, in the eighteenth and especially nineteenth centuries, and had more broadly European origins. The idea that nature had to be protected against native improvidence and destructiveness became yet another justification for imperial rule and resulted in further land seizures. Many state conservation agencies in the now-independent South trace their origins to colonial bureaucracies. Indeed, British ideas about property and conservation were developed substantially with reference to (and sometimes in) the colonies, especially Ireland, India and the Americas.

The concern of people in the North with the regulation of land rights and conservation in the South thus goes back a long way. I argue here that a new era for both concerns began in the 1970s as a familiar list of transnational actors – northern states (especially through their development agencies) IFIs, international NGOs and private corporations – intensified their engagement, committing large amounts of money and resources to titling and conservation projects. These interventions have been shaped by powerful global discourses that tell us how things should be done with respect to land rights and the environment. Such discourses claim that conservation areas are vital to the preservation of the local, national and global environments, and that titling is an indispensable part of the prescription for prosperity and the incorporation of poor people into full national citizenship. The goals that motivate these actors and are expressed in these discourses should primarily be understood, again, in terms of the will to improve. Even with these motivations, however, transnational proponents of titling and conservation are inevitably involved in a push for control, and at times (especially in the case of conservation) in actual grabs for land. Transnational actors seek, in all kinds of overt ways, to change the regulations that govern land in the South, and in some cases to help determine who gets property rights to what land.

Titling

Large amounts of land in the South (and in formerly socialist countries) are not effectively subject to formal, state-backed property rights. In these countries, much land – both rural and urban – is held under more informal arrangements in which organizations and powerful figures at the neighbourhood, village or other relatively local levels play an important role in regulating land use and property. Often, these customary arrangements (see chapter 4) exist in shifting and uneasy combination with state-backed property systems, so it can be a mistake to draw too strong a distinction between 'local/ customary' and 'formal/state-backed' regulation. The fact that land is locally governed does not necessarily mean that it is held in common. Huge numbers of households across the South hold and use their land more or less as private property but lack effective state-backed documents verifying that the land is theirs. The process by which informal property claims and systems of regulating land use are recorded by state officials and incorporated into the formal legal system is referred to as *formalization*. Formalization can take many forms and apply to diverse types of property claims. Formal state recognition of collective rights to forests, pasturelands, swamps, fishing grounds and other common property areas, for instance, has been a central part of development policy for several decades. Even individual property rights may be formalized in ways that limit the rights recognized: the right to transfer the land may not be included, or landholding may be restricted to members of a certain ethnic group.

Titling is a particular kind of formalization, one often seen as formalization's logical conclusion. Titling is usually seen to give 'full' private property rights to land, including ownership, the right to exclude people from the land and the right of alienation, that is, the right to transfer the land by sale, inheritance or as a gift. While there are varying legal frameworks for title, titling projects generally involve three main elements. First, plots of land are measured and recorded in a central registry known as a cadastre. Second, the ownership of each plot is recorded and the owner receives a title deed. Ownership details are supposed to be updated when the land is transferred. Third, titling projects may also involve changes to legal and administrative systems when the legal infrastructure for titling is defective or does not exist. A (usually explicit) goal of such changes is that the new system will replace other systems for regulating property rights. Rather than co-existing or overlapping with other tenure regimes, the formal legal system is meant to be the sole authoritative source of information about property and the sole authoritative mechanism for resolving conflicts over it. Again, titling is not the same as the individualization or privatization of land; rather, it is the extension of a particular type of state recognition of property rights. As all this implies, titling projects in the South have an important institution-building component. They seek to strengthen, if not to transform, the formal legal and administrative structures responsible for regulating property in land.

The case for titling involves a long series of interlinked

arguments, and different people and organizations stress some elements over others. One of the most emphasized benefits of a formal and effective system of title is that it protects people's property against predation and seizure by other actors (including actors within the state). Title, that is, gives tenure security. Second, this secure claim is widely argued in mainstream development thinking to stimulate investment in land. People who feel assured that their land will not be seized, the argument goes, will have a stronger incentive to invest in improvements to the land because they know they will receive the benefits from them. Third, titling is said to make it easier for people to use their land as collateral when seeking a loan because the formal, effective claim that title embodies will reassure lenders that they will be able to take possession of the land if the borrower defaults. This claim is controversial even for many proponents of titling, however, and evidence that poor farmers have been able or willing to use their land as collateral is scanty.

A fourth purported benefit of titling is that the incorporation of a property into a unified system of representation should make it easier to buy and sell the land (or parts of it) because, as an influential World Bank publication on land rights put it, 'broadly recognized property rights facilitate abstract representation and impersonal exchange of rights, thereby increasing the scope for exchange with outsiders.'[2] This is meant to be good both for the owners, in that it makes it easier for them to sell their land should they wish to and to get a fair price for it, and for the national economy, as it supposedly facilitates the transfer of land to the most efficient user (defined as the potential user willing to pay the most for it) through 'willing buyer, willing seller' transactions on the free market. All four of these effects of titling – tenure security, increased investment in the land, the ability to use land as collateral and lubricated land markets – are seen by proponents as likely to raise the value of the newly titled land, and thus of a critical asset held by the poor.

Other arguments for titling are less directly market-oriented. It is often suggested that titling holds out the promise of improving the status and independence of women by giving them legal ownership of property. Titling is also widely claimed to have environmental benefits on the grounds that the higher value of titled land and the more efficient and intensive use that farmers make of it will encourage them to stay put rather than moving into the forest in search of new land. There is also a set of propositions that see titling as having beneficial consequences for the state, the nation, and democracy. The heightened legibility (see chapter 3) that titling brings makes it easier for the state to tax land and to regulate its use for the public good. More profoundly, it is argued that protecting the assets of the poor, and incorporating them into a properly functioning and fair legal system, brings them into the fold of genuine citizenship and is thus an act of nation-building. Indeed, a final, simple argument in titling's favour, and one with substantial (though not universal) empirical support, is that people want it. Most people would like to have formal state recognition that they are the owners of the property they consider theirs.

Two caveats to these arguments about titling should be noted. First, even committed advocates of titling who accept most or all of the propositions in the previous two paragraphs do not usually claim that full titling is always the best approach. Most proponents, including the World Bank, see collective or communal land ownership as more appropriate under some circumstances. Titling, again, is said to work best under conditions in which people already hold their land more or less as individual private property but lack formal recognition of their rights. A second caveat is that even people who accept the logic of some of the claims advanced above may view the posited outcomes as negative. 'Better functioning' land markets have been seen as facilitating dispossession, as people in distress sell land, rather than increased prosperity for farmers and smoother exits from agriculture. The higher land values that titling supposedly leads to are not likely to be a plus for farmers who rent or for the landless. The heightened information about land that titling gives the state – titling's legibility effect – may lead to intensified state demands for revenue and, in the worst cases, may make the land more 'visible' to actors who wish to seize it (with the cadastral register serving as a Sears catalogue for land grabbers).

While the arguments surveyed above are emphasized to varying degrees by proponents of titling, together they constitute a powerful discourse and a central pillar of contemporary neoliberal development policy. This discourse has been vigorously promoted in the reports of international organizations and national development agencies and by a number of influential 'policy entrepreneurs'. Particularly prominent among the latter is the Peruvian economist Hernando de Soto, whose 2000 book *The Mystery of Capital: Why Capitalism Triumphs in the West and Fails Everywhere Else* makes an impassioned and compellingly written case for understanding formalized property rights as the primary cause of economic growth.[3] De Soto's ideas have been enormously influential since the 1990s and have been championed by such well-known figures as Bill Clinton. The organization that de Soto heads, the Institute for Liberty and Democracy (ILD), has carried out research, advocacy and on-the-ground projects designed to bring de Soto's vision into being. The ILD's website states that its mission is

> to help developing countries make fundamental institutional changes regarding their property and business environments, encouraging people to enter the legal system and offering them as an incentive those essential legal tools that will not only improve their lives and businesses, but also

help them transform their society: fungible property rights, forms to organize their businesses and mechanisms to access expanded markets, nationally and internationally.[4]

De Soto's ideas have also been spread by the United Nations Development Project's Commission on Legal Empowerment of the Poor, which was chaired by de Soto and former US Secretary of State Madeleine Albright and laid out an extremely ambitious agenda for extending the full protection of national legal systems to the four billion people that the Commission argued are excluded from them. They have also been championed in populist terms by politicians across the South, and the ILD claims that 29 heads of state have sought its advice on legal reform. The power of discourses around land titling and formalization also extends to the work of major development organizations, notably the World Bank. The Bank has produced a number of widely read studies on land policy that highlight titling, including Klaus Deininger's 2003 book, *Land Policies for Growth and Poverty Reduction*.[5]

Titling as a political project is backed up by more than the persuasive arguments of charismatic transnational policy entrepreneurs. Huge amounts of transnational money and effort have gone into promoting titling (in addition, again, to other kinds of formalization that do not involve full title). IFIs like the World Bank, national development agencies like USAID, AusAID, Germany's GTZ and the Millennium Challenge Corporation, and non-governmental organizations such as CARE and the ILD, have energetically funded and assisted in the implementation of on-the-ground titling projects. Private corporations, like the Australian firm Land Equity International, have also been involved in such projects. Some of the efforts have been massive. The World Bank–AusAID Land Titling Project in Thailand, which was established in 1984 to work with Thailand's Department of Lands, had by 1998 raised the number of title deeds in the country from 4 million to roughly 13 million. The success of this project has long made Thailand the World Bank's star pupil when it comes to titling. By 1996, the World Bank had land titling and registration projects on the go in Algeria, Argentina, Bolivia, El Salvador, Indonesia, Lao PDR, Lebanon, Nicaragua, Papua New Guinea (PNG), Paraguay, Russia, Venezuela and Thailand, and was preparing projects in ten other countries.[6]

There is a basic tension at the heart of the land titling push. The neoliberal discourse about titling and formalization presented by de Soto, Deininger and others, and put into practice in dozens of development projects, has a number of highly persuasive elements. The ideas that the poor should be protected by the formal legal system and secure from land seizure are difficult to oppose. Many advocates of titling, too, state that their goal is to recognize not just the rights of the poor in general, but the systems of property rights regulation developed by the poor. The ILD and de Soto, in particular, take pains to emphasize that they are not seeking to impose a one-size-fits-all template, but rather to adopt a 'bottom-up' approach that recognizes and builds upon existing property rights and existing systems of adjudicating them. Often, proponents of titling argue that their interventions do not alter existing rights and claims but only provide formal legal recognition of them.

At the same time, however, titling involves a profound project of state transformation, with goals that include changing the legal system, reshaping administration, surveying vast amounts of land, issuing millions of title deeds and changing the fundamental political economy of the country's legal system and land relations in such a way that all the other changes will actually stick. The range of ways in which this can be done is not infinite; rather, the goals, and many of the methods, are known from the beginning. Projects must incorporate the criteria, the aims and the methods laid down by outside experts who claim the expertise, on the basis of theory, empirical evidence and existing 'best practice', to know how development works. At the same time as the ILD emphasizes that it takes a 'bottom-up' approach to formalization, it also claims to be in possession of 'a new and powerful way of examining a developing economy – to see what works and what doesn't, what practices have to be scrapped and what can be built upon'. The paradoxical message – as so often in development policy – thus seems to be: we want you to do exactly what you want to do, but to do it using the methods, and in pursuit of the goals, that we experts know are best. De Soto and the World Bank may be correct in asserting that their approach to land policy is the best one, and they are pursuing this issue because they genuinely believe that to be the case – that is, because of their will to improve. But it is very hard not to see this as a push for control over the basic legal and administrative mechanisms by which property in land is regulated in other countries. A villager quoted in a study of the Land Titling Project for Small Farmers established by the government of Honduras and USAID in the early 1980s succinctly summed up the matter by saying of the project: 'Everything comes copied.'[7]

How, then, do titling projects actually change control over land? What are their results with respect to regulation and property, to who gets what and how? What can we learn from detailed case studies and ethnographic accounts of titling?[8] Perceived outcomes range from the good to the dreadful. Advocates of titling often point to the Thai case as a success story, while the literature on Latin America includes some very distressing findings. These differences are rooted not just in the different ways in which projects have been organized, but in the nature of the existing local and national political economies. Within the diversity, a number of points that work against the pro-titling discourse stand out. First, the purported benefits of titling for women are by no means universal. In many cases, women have lost access to land they previously had some claim to when title was issued only in the name of their husbands. Some studies have also found that titling projects do not inquire deeply into the conditions under which current landholders came to occupy their land, and thus provide state-backed legitimation for early land grabs. Indeed, one of the basic premises of land titling projects – that they do not seek to adjudicate or change existing property rights, only to formalize them – suggests that this would be a likely outcome.

Titling projects can also stimulate *new* grabs for land as the promise of state recognition for claims prompts powerful actors to take possession of as much as they can before the surveyors show up. One study found that the 'first tangible result' of the announcement of a project to formalize customary rights in Niger was 'a massive upsurge of conflicts between competing right holders all attempting to position themselves most favourably for when the reform eventually would be adopted'.[9] Titling mechanisms may also be more accessible for the rich than for the poor, in part because titling is expensive. Landholders may need to pay a fee to have the land surveyed, another to receive title to it and another when they transfer the land to someone else (all in addition to new taxes that may be levied when the land becomes 'visible' to the state). While development projects obviously provide financial support for titling schemes, they generally do so by means of loans that the state will eventually need to repay. The USAID-funded project in Honduras mentioned above provides a particularly dispiriting example. In this instance, people who received loans in order to get their land titled during the first phase of the project were then, in a second phase, threatened with eviction if they could not repay their debt. In a painful irony, receipt of title had made people *more* vulnerable to eviction by the state.[10]

This last argument suggests a further tension in the case for titling. Titling projects are expensive, difficult to undertake and perhaps even more difficult to maintain. Land-registration projects identify weak and unresponsive legal and administrative systems as problems to be fixed. But in a situation of weak state capacity, titling projects will likely be carried out haphazardly (tardiness and incompleteness of implementation are constant themes in the literature) and not be followed up on. They thus run the risk of becoming empty institutions: rules and systems that sit on the statute books but that no one follows. The 1980s was not the first decade in which it ever occurred to anyone to title land in the South. There are millions of ancient title documents quietly gathering dust in cupboards across Africa, Asia and Latin America, relics of titling projects that did not stick. The problem that titling projects confront is sometimes not a lack of state recognition for land rights but a *surfeit* of it, in the form of multiple, conflicting title documents for the same land stretching back a hundred years or more. In the area of rural Honduras mentioned above, twentieth-century processes of land redistribution have left 'a large variety of documents and claims' as their legacy. What, then, will make things different this time? For titling to work, there must be a high level of state capacity and commitment, and people must see that applying for title (which costs money) and recording land transfers (for which a fee is also paid) are in their interests, are something worth doing. They need to make that decision, often, in the face of primarily negative experiences of the state and the legal system as sources of, not solutions to, predation. Titling projects thus seem to assume the existence of a capable and reasonably fair state at the same time that they posit the absence of such a state as the problem to be solved.

It is also important, in thinking about who controls land, to be careful of overly sharp distinctions between 'local' and 'state' forms of regulation. Both proponents and opponents of title tend to assume that titling projects counterpose formal state law to informal local custom, with the latter pristine and 'traditional'. But in fact 'local' practices often integrate or interact with state law, including prior, overlapping efforts at providing title. People may, for instance, look to local leaders or groups for adjudication of conflicts over land boundaries, while also holding on to receipts for land taxes paid as evidence that the state has recognized their presence on their land. As chapter 3 demonstrated, too, 'local' leaders, such as the *maliks* of FATA, may have their authority in large part because of their relationship with the state. If existing land governance is in fact a complex mix of local and state-backed practices deriving from different historical periods and modified to fit the conditions at hand, adding another layer of partially implemented and fitfully followed-up title documents can *increase*, rather than reduce, complexity and uncertainty around land, and thus make tenure *less* secure. Such outcomes change social and political-economic relations, and thus contradict the argument that land formalization projects simply recognize pre-existing rights. Indeed, this is true more generally: to formalize rights is to change them and the way they are regulated, and simply 'recognizing what exists' is impossible. Even when titling projects are not seized on by the powerful to dispossess current landholders (as happens in the worst cases), then, titling often leads to more rather than less confusion over land rights and who governs them.

What conclusions can be drawn from all this? The first (somewhat perversely) is that an overall conclusion is difficult to draw. While there is certainly a global expansion in the amount of land covered by title, what that really means in any given place – more or less tenure security, certainty, land market activity, rights for women and so on – cannot be determined without detailed local research. We thus find ourselves back in the 'frontier' conditions of chapter 3 in two respects. One is that we have seen that lack of full state authority over land regulation is not limited to 'frontiers' far from centres of power. Indeed, as de Soto emphasizes, some of the areas where land relations are most marked by informality and the absence of an effective state presence are the slum and peri-urban districts that surround major cities and may be only a short distance from the national parliament or the core business district. The other is that while it is tempting, when considering the long sweep of history, to argue that the amount of land effectively governed by 'the state' is inexorably increasing, we do need to recall the enormous local variation that characterizes the outcomes of titling projects.

Conservation

The conservationist rationale for intervening in land-use regulation and property rights allocation is, at its heart, very simple. It states that human activity is doing irreparable harm to nature or the environment, that it is imperative that this damage be halted or reversed and that, in order for nature to be protected, human land-use patterns need to change. Conservationists argue that in the face of processes like deforestation, desertification, urbanization and agricultural expansion, and the losses in biodiversity that result from them, at least some control over land use must be exerted. In most countries, all land is subject to at least some conservationist regulation, for instance through prohibitions on harvesting or killing certain species of plants or animals. In this chapter, however, the focus is on land that has been specifically zoned as some form of protected area. When land is zoned in this way, conservation frequently becomes a matter not just of changing the way land is regulated but of changing its status as property.

The International Union for Conservation of Nature (IUCN) defines a protected area as a 'clearly defined geographical space, recognized, dedicated and managed, through legal or other effective means, to achieve the long term conservation of nature with associated ecosystem and cultural values'.[11] This category encompasses a range both of rationales for and of types and intensities of protection. The IUCN divides protected areas into seven types:

Ia   Strict Nature Reserve
Ib   Wilderness Area
II   National Park
III   Natural Monument or Feature
IV   Habitat/Species Management Area
V   Protected Landscape/Seascape
VI   Protected Area with Sustainable Use of Natural Resources

Protected areas account for a huge and rapidly growing amount of the world's surface. Figure 5.1 and Table 5.1 give statistics collected by the World Database on Protected Areas (WDPA), a collaborative project of the IUCN, United Nations Environment Programme (UNEP) and the World Conservation Monitoring Centre (WCMC).[12] The graph shows growth since 1911 in the area of terrestrial and marine protected areas. The great majority of the growth in terrestrial protected area has occurred since 1960, and by 2011 the WDPA listed more than 16 million km² of land as protected. Table 5.1 gives a regional breakdown of growth in protected land area between 1990 and 2010, and shows that by the latter date Latin America and the Caribbean, Eastern Asia and Western Asia all had more than 15 per cent of their land under protected status.

There are reasons to be sceptical about these figures, as indeed there are for any global statistics on land regulation. One involves the enormous difficulty of collecting accurate

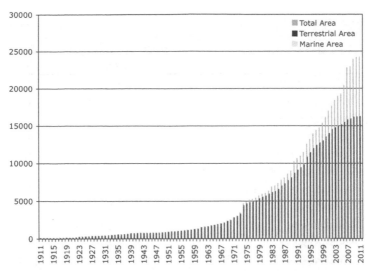

Figure 5.1 Growth in nationally designated protected areas (thousands of km²), 1911–2011

and comparable data on the world's tens of thousands of protected areas. Another is that the WDPA reports only on 'nationally designated' protected areas, ignoring, for instance, areas that have been protected by villages or other local groups, and private land that has been declared a protected area by the owners (including game preserves and the tracts of land bought up by conservationist NGOs like the Nature Conservancy). A third is that many protected areas have that status in law only, while in practice there are few effective limits on their use – that is, they are 'paper parks'. Even with these caveats, however, the fact that states have moved to protect areas of their territory that add up to more than the total land area of Russia is remarkable.

Conservation is a transnational project. A central reason is that, while most of the money and powerful interests in favour of conservation are in the North, many of the ecosystems and

Table 5.1 Percentage of terrestrial area protected, by region, 1990 and 2010

	1990	2010
World (outside Antarctica)	8.8	12.7
Developed Regions	8.7	11.6
Developing Regions	8.8	13.3
Northern Africa	3.3	4.0
Sub-Saharan Africa	11.1	11.8
Latin America and the Caribbean	9.7	20.3
Caucasus and Central Asia	2.7	3.0
Eastern Asia	12.0	15.9
Southern Asia	5.3	6.2
South-East Asia	8.7	13.8
Western Asia	3.8	15.4
Oceania	2.0	4.9

much of the biodiversity deemed to be in most critical need of protection are in the South. Tropical forests, which are home to enormous numbers of species and play a critical role in regulating the global climate, are the iconic southern ecosystems in this respect. When species and ecosystems in the South are taken to be irreplaceable parts of the 'global commons' or of humanity's 'common heritage', and when harms done to them are seen to negatively affect people everywhere, then actors in the North will work to save them, and indeed may feel a moral imperative to do so. These kinds of cross-border relationships are not all North–South. Europeans have worked very hard to stop the Canadian seal hunt, as Canadians work to prevent Japanese from whaling. International environmental treaties are meant to be negotiated by all states and to bind all their signatories. The North–South connections, however, stand out because of their extent, because of the argument that nature in the South is both critically important for biodiversity purposes and unusually threatened because of poverty and weak governance and because of the imbalances in resources and power that North–South relationships so often involve. (There are, as far as I am aware, no Kenyan-funded nature reserves in Germany or Indonesian-designed resource-management projects in the United States.) While conservationist interventions in the South are justified at different scales – as being for the good of the planet or humanity, or of the people who live in the vicinity of the nature under threat – they are tied together by the interest Northern actors take in shaping land regulation and property in the South, by their concern to modify the ways in which land may, may not and must be used – and who has the right to use it.

Transnational conservation has a number of strands. One important element is the ensemble of conservationist treaties and conventions that states have created, many of them through the United Nations system. Key examples include the Convention on Biological Diversity, the Kyoto Protocol and the Convention on International Trade in Endangered Species of Wild Fauna and Flora (CITES). Most of these conventions have spatial components and implications, and some have the demarcation and protection of land as their central focus. The concept of the world's 'common heritage', for instance, is made very concrete by the UNESCO World Heritage Convention, which has recognized 725 cultural, 183 natural and 28 'mixed' sites as World Heritage Sites. The Ramsar Convention on Wetlands, similarly, had as of October 2011 designated 1,952 sites, covering over 190 million hectares, as Wetlands of International Importance. The 160 member states have committed to the 'three pillars' of the Convention, which are:

> to designate suitable wetlands for the List of Wetlands of International Importance [. . .] and ensure their effective

management; to work towards the wise use of all their wet-lands through national land-use planning, appropriate policies and legislation, management actions, and public education; and to cooperate internationally concerning trans-boundary wetlands, shared wetland systems, shared species, and development projects that may affect wetlands.[13]

Such conventions, then, create a globally sanctioned set of criteria that contracting parties have agreed to incorporate into their regulations on land use.

In what follows, I highlight two sets of northern actors engaged in transnational conservation: NGOs based in the North (international NGOs hereafter) and donor organizations (both the bilateral aid agencies of national governments and multilateral donors such as the World Bank). International NGOs and donors often work together, and they derive substantial power from their resources of knowledge and money. While large numbers of conservationist NGOs work internationally, the focus here will be on a small group of what are often called BINGOs, or Big International NGOs. Organizations like the World Wide Fund for Nature (WWF), the Nature Conservancy, Conservation International and the Wildlife Conservation Society are substantial concerns, with budgets in the tens if not hundreds of millions of dollars per year and activities in many countries. Bilateral and multilateral donors, meanwhile, were once associated with conservation primarily through the environmental damage done by their projects, but since the 1980s they have increasingly prioritized conservationist goals. They have done this most obviously by directly funding conservation (including by funding NGOs, whether international ones based in the North or those in the country where the project is being carried out). They have also, however, incorporated conservationist regulation into their non-environmental aid (a process known as 'green conditionality'). For example, donors may require that environmental damage done by their funded projects be mitigated, perhaps by planting trees elsewhere to compensate for those cut down in building a road or a dam. There is substantial overlap and mutual support in the approaches to conservation taken by the BINGOs and the main donor agencies, and the models and forms of 'best practice' they have devised are influential well beyond the projects they directly fund.

How do northern actors engage in conservation in the South, and what kinds of alliances do they build with people in the countries they seek to affect? We can identify three basic stances. In the first, northern actors ally primarily with state officials to create and support parks that exclude local people from access, an approach often referred to as 'fortress conservation'. In the second, they see the 'local' people who use and rely on the resource or habitat in question as capable of managing and conserving it, but argue that their management needs to be assisted and improved, notably through projects promoting community-based natural resource management (CBNRM). The third stance, which is more politically radical and is associated with smaller and more oppositional groups, sees northerners seek to make common cause with the people living in a threatened area against the state agencies, corporations and/or migrants who threaten both to displace them and to degrade the environment. In this approach, the people in the area are often seen as already in sustainable interaction with the environment, and their resource management is not seen to be the problem (though it may be in need of support); the threat, rather, is from the outside, from the encroaching forces of capitalism and development, from states, markets and modernity. While I focus on the first two forms of engagement below, we can note again that all three stances are united by the desire of northern actors to shape how land is used and controlled, and who uses and controls it, in other countries.

The 'fortress conservation' or 'parks without people'

approach has its roots both in the national parks movement in the United States and in European imperial practices of reserving forests for future harvesting. The vision is that parks should be places where 'wild' nature is left alone, places off limits to human exploitation and habitation. In some cases, making this happen requires that the people already living in the park area be evicted, and that measures (including fencing and surveillance) be taken to keep them and other potential users out of it. Conservation zones also need to be delimited and formalized through processes quite similar to those involved in titling. Such an approach is the flip side of the environmental motivations behind land titling discussed above in that the goal is to draw a clear distinction between titled land open for exploitation and protected areas where nature can do its own thing.

The 'fortress conservation' approach sees local people primarily as a threat to nature and is often unapologetic about evicting them or using force to keep new 'encroachers' or 'squatters' out. In response to the charge that the land that now makes up Yellowstone and other American national parks was originally stolen from either Native Americans or from the white people who had taken the land from them, prominent conservationist Richard Leakey replied, 'you know, one has to say, thank God someone *did* think of stealing this land from somebody else, because if they hadn't we wouldn't have it today. That's the bottom line, isn't it?'[14] Supporters of 'fortress conservation' may also argue, however, that, while nature needs to be protected from people, the people evicted from or prevented from accessing the park deserve compensation – and, more pragmatically, that if they are not helped to develop new sources of livelihood they will likely jeopardize the park by continuing to use it. Integrated conservation and development projects (ICDPs) have, since the 1980s, sought to create such new sources of livelihood, often through the development of tourism and other park-related industries. A final important point here is that 'parks without people' does not mean that no people at all will have access to the park; rather, a new group of people associated with conservation gets access. As Dan Brockington, Rosaleen Duffy and Jim Igoe put it, such parks see 'the physical displacement of generally poor rural people to make way for spaces that are then occupied by the transnational leisure industry, wealthy tourists, research scientists and conservation NGOs', and of course state officials and guards.[15] The dollar value of the goods and services generated from the park may actually increase after such 'green grabs', but the money goes to very different people.

A second approach, which involves supporting natural resource management by 'communities', works quite differently. One point of entry into this approach is the observation that few, if any, terrestrial environments have come to be what they are in the absence of human intervention. Even the great symbols of 'wild', 'pristine', 'untouched' nature, areas like the Amazon rainforest, are in fact anthropogenic: they have developed in interaction with and have been profoundly shaped by humans over thousands of years. Viewed from this perspective, conservationist arguments that protecting nature requires that it be kept off limits to humans make little sense. Many ecosystems have in fact been destabilized by the exclusion of humans from them. Proponents of CBNRM draw on, and seek to support, the ways in which the users of natural resources have formed institutions and rules to govern their interactions with them and preserve them. Compared to 'fortress conservation', the discourse here is much more likely to be win–win. Rather than seeing locals as the main threat to the preservation of nature, and arguing that sacrifices need to be made locally in order for globally important values to be preserved, CBNRM projects argue that the people who rely on the resource are best positioned to preserve it.

The design and implementation of CBNRM programmes, however, again raise difficult questions about transnational control over land use. CBNRM projects do not generally argue that communities are already managing resources sustainably and simply need to be given more resources to keep on doing what they are doing. As Tania Murray Li puts it in her discussion of community forest management as an 'assemblage', 'This is not an assemblage in which anything goes.'[16] Rather, such projects take 'community' to be both already present and in need of creation, modification and improvement. They focus on developing new institutions and promoting models of 'best practice'. Community activities must conform to criteria for funding (including participation), and must generate 'outputs' that donors can point to when projects are audited or come up for renewal. 'Communities' and local NGOs find that they need to conform to, or at least to perform, the criteria prioritized by donors if their activities are to be recognized, supported and funded, and if they are to maintain access to the resource in question. The will to improve, in other words, is still at work. To say this is not necessarily to criticize CBNRM. The whole point of an intervention is to make a difference to the way things work in pursuit of certain goals – otherwise why would donors or NGOs intervene in the first place? It is simply to recognize that CBNRM seeks to transform land use in the South in a context in which relevant resources of money and knowledge are concentrated in the North.

Hundreds if not thousands of protected areas and conservation projects could illustrate the ways transnational actors seek to influence land-use regulation and property rights for conservation purposes. The interactions documented by Paige West in her 2007 book *Conservation is our Government Now: The Politics of Ecology in Papua New Guinea* provide one window onto these processes.[17] West gives a rich account of the varied and conflicting understandings of conservation, development and social relations held by the people engaged with the area of highland Papua New Guinea in which she worked, and her emphasis on conservation's contested history (including different accounts of who agreed to what when) makes her work difficult to summarize. We can, however, establish some of the basics. David Gillison, the husband of an anthropologist doing fieldwork in PNG, became the first foreigner to concern himself with conservation in the area called Maimafu when he took an interest in birds of paradise in the late 1970s. Gillison worked with local men to implement various conservation-oriented initiatives funded from outside PNG, including an early ecotourism project. In 1994, Maimafu was incorporated into the 2,690 km² Crater Mountain Wildlife Management Area (CMWMA). A foreign employee of the Wildlife Conservation Society (WCS), an American NGO, participated in the state delineation of the CMWMA. During this formalization process, landholders were helped to establish the boundaries of their land and to decide who would be on the Wildlife Management Committees, which are 'made up of representative members of clans from the bounded area who will work with the state to codify boundaries and rules'. The CMWMA and the people who lived in it also became part of an externally funded integrated conservation and development project that ran from 1994 to 1999. Under this project, West writes, 'it was promised that if Gimi and Pawaia gave their lands for inclusion in the Wildlife Management Area, they would derive cash benefits, access to economic markets for the forest products tied to local biological diversity, and "development".'

The organizations involved in creating the ICDP constituted a complex and well-funded mix, spanning the private–public and the foreign–local divides. The main donor for the Crater Project was the Biodiversity Conservation Network (BCN), which provided almost US$500,000 between 1995 and 1998;

the WCS also gave US$76,590. The BCN, in turn, was created in 1992 out of a collaboration between the Biodiversity Support Program (BSP) (itself a consortium of the WWF, the Nature Conservancy and the World Resources Institute) and USAID, the US government's bilateral development arm. In 1992, USAID had provided the BCN with US$20 million in order to undertake projects that would test, in the BSP's words, 'the hypothesis that if local communities receive sufficient benefits from a biodiversity-linked enterprise, then they will act to conserve' biodiversity. The project was designed and implemented by three NGOs staffed by people from the US, Australia and PNG, with conceptual design supported by a BCN grant and help from BCN staff. Project administration was carried out by the Research and Conservation Foundation of Papua New Guinea (RCF), an NGO that Gillison had founded and that had been incorporated in 1986 with the help of the WCS and PNG's Department of Environment and Conservation. The RCF ran various projects in the CMWMA that were meant to bring together the objectives of conservation and development.

While West's book does not give the impression that there were any areas of the CMWMA from which villagers were completely excluded, villagers felt strongly that they had contributed both their land and labour to the project, and the project's goals included developing new laws about land use that would alter their hunting and tree-cutting behaviour. As West writes, the 'projects were at their base about changing the actions and practices of local people in order to meet the end goal of conservation.' West documents a number of striking consequences of the creation of the CMWMA and the implementation of the Crater Project, including the way that villagers have come to look to the RCF for adjudication of their property claims. More broadly, she shows repeatedly that the Gimi people in the area felt that, because the project sought to bring about the development that used to be promised (but was never delivered) by the state, the project was now the government (hence the title of the book). She also shows that most villagers feel strongly that others are benefiting from their conservation actions while development remains out of reach for them. As some of the villagers put it, 'We are like a fence around a garden. We have worked to keep people out and to keep things right, and now there are things growing inside. Who is eating the food in our garden? Us or RCF? What are we getting out of this relationship?'

The discussion above has tried to give a sense of the tensions and conundrums that exist when northern conservationists seek to exercise control over land-use regulation and property rights in order to 'protect' nature in the South. As in the case of titling projects, however, international conservation should not be understood as some kind of juggernaut, as always getting its way. Both 'fortress conservation' and CBNRM are as notable for their failures as for anything else. Much of the urgency that conservationists feel around protected areas derives precisely from their relative lack of success in moving beyond 'paper parks'. Indeed, titling and conservation can be quite similar in this respect. When I was an undergraduate in Canada in the early 1990s, I was given an acre of rainforest as a Christmas present. I don't remember where the land was located (I think it was somewhere in Central America), but I do remember receiving a certificate stating that this land would be preserved by an international NGO in my name. Conservation and titling were connected here by the idea that individuals in the North could protect forests in the South by buying land through the good offices of an NGO. I have no idea what has happened to that land. Like millions of people throughout the South, though, I'm pretty sure I still have the certificate documenting my claim in a drawer somewhere.

Conclusion

This has been the second of two chapters addressing transnational efforts to 'improve' land regulation and property in
land in the South. My analyses of land titling (and formalization more broadly) and conservation have engaged with the
questions of what people may, may not and must do with their
land, how their holding of it is governed and who actually gets
what rights to it. I have focused on titling and conservation
because of the key transnational role in both and because
of the sheer number of people affected by these processes.
Titling and conservation are often seen to be the inverse of one
another: titled land is for productive use, protected areas are
for conservation, and the clear demarcation and effective governance of one is said to make the other work more smoothly.
My goal has not been to criticize these projects, which often
have positive effects and are for the most part motivated by a
real desire to make the world a better place. However, I have
shown that both projects by definition involve a transnational
push for influence and control over land in the South, and that
both can have negative as well as positive consequences. The
period since the 1970s has thus seen an intensifying transnational role in some of the most day-to-day, 'local' aspects of
people's relationship with land in the South.

CHAPTER SIX

Social Movements

This chapter explores the social movement activism of indigenous peoples and small-scale farmers around land. While the politics of land have been a constant theme in this book, the ways in which people mobilize around land, and the ways in which activism simultaneously engages issues of territory, regulation and property, demand focused attention. Indigenous and agrarian activism is taking place in the context of, and in response to, the pressures on rural land (and rural people) discussed in the preceding chapters. Among these are: rising state and corporate demand for rural land for a variety of purposes, including urban development, export-oriented agriculture, infrastructure and conservation; intensified efforts to exert regulatory control over land in the areas of property-rights governance and conservation; and state drives to bring frontier land under firmer territorial control. As Philip Hirsch, Tania Murray Li and I argued in the South East Asian context in our book *Powers of Exclusion*, rural people are being excluded from access to land through the interplay of regulations, market dynamics, legitimating discourses about land's proper use, and force and the threat of force. In the introduction to this chapter, I expand further on the context for land-related social movements by examining the place of land in indigenous mobilization, and the day-to-day economic pressures faced by small-scale farmers in the South.

The second part of the chapter analyses the rise of

transnational indigenous and agrarian movements. Since the 1970s, transnational indigenous organizing has become a prominent and, in many ways, novel element of world politics. One of the most striking consequences has been the adoption by the UN General Assembly (on a vote of 143 in favour against four opposed), on 13 September 2007, of the UN Declaration on the Rights of Indigenous Peoples. UNDRIP has substantial implications for indigenous rights over land in terms of territory, regulation and property. The main contemporary transnational agrarian movements, meanwhile, emerged in the 1990s. Movements like La Vía Campesina have engaged in international campaigns around land, including a push against market-led agrarian reform, the promotion of a UN declaration on peasant rights and opposition to the global land grab. I make a set of arguments regarding the reasons for the expansion of transnational activism around land and reflect on what these movements have and have not been able to achieve.

The chapter then turns to contention around land conversion and dispossession at China's rural–urban fringe, processes driven by political dynamics and economic goals that are in some respects quite similar to those discussed with respect to India in chapter 4. This is an important case for this book for three reasons. First, the scale of Chinese urbanization, and the implications of the process for land relations and dispossession, beggar belief. One estimate suggests that between 1990 and 2002, over 50 million Chinese peasants had some or all of their land seized. Second, the extent of peasant protest in China and the particular form that it has taken are striking, and I examine the reasons for both. Third, the transnational component in this case is in fact quite limited. While some of China's industrial zones are aimed at attracting FDI, and while transnational discourses are again influential here, activism around land in China takes place almost entirely at the national and sub-national levels. This reminder of the centrality of the local and the national in the context of what is arguably the most important land-related dynamic taking place in a single country anywhere in the world in the early twenty-first century is an appropriate place to close a book on the transnational element in land relations.

Indigenous and farmer activism: context and pressures

Indigenous peoples and small-scale farmers in the South face many of the same pressures around land. While it is difficult to generalize about the situations and goals of such large and diverse groups, I try to establish some context here. Relationships between states and indigenous peoples have been marked by centuries of colonialism, racism, displacement, expropriation and/or use of land without indigenous consent, and paternalism, including formal systems of law and administration that distinguish indigenous peoples from dominant populations. The recently intensified state and corporate drive for land for large-scale agriculture, natural resource extraction and forestry has also fallen especially heavily on indigenous peoples, who often live on land that is prioritized for such projects (partly, of course, on the grounds that it is sparsely populated and 'under-utilized', and needs to be brought into the mainstream of the national economy). Recent decades have also seen moves towards national and international recognition of indigenous land rights and some elements of self-determination, and one result of this has been a trend towards indigenous groups partnering with states and corporations in natural resource development projects (as seen in chapters 3 and 4).

Much indigenous mobilization and activism is also based on a radically different sense of land than that expressed in dominant conceptions of state territory, private property and land as a natural resource. This understanding is expressed in the following two quotations, the first of which refers to indigenous peoples as 'they', the second as 'we'. The first is from the United Nations Department of Economic and Social Affairs' 2009 report *State of the World's Indigenous Peoples*:

> The importance of land and territories to indigenous cultural identity cannot be stressed enough. The survival and development of indigenous peoples' particular ways of life, their traditional knowledge, their handicrafts and other cultural expressions have, since time immemorial, depended on their access and rights to their traditional lands, territories and natural resources. But land is not only the basis of the indigenous economy. Indigenous peoples also have a deep spiritual relationship with the land; they feel at one with their ancestral territory and feel responsible for the healthy maintenance of the land – its waters and soils, its plants and animals – for both themselves and future generations. Land is where their ancestors are buried and where sacred places are visited and revered.[1]

The second contains excerpts from the 2010 Indigenous Peoples' Declaration that emerged from the Indigenous Peoples Working Group of the World People's Conference on Climate Change and the Rights of Mother Earth. The Declaration was subtitled 'Mother Earth can live without us, but we can't live without her.' Among the statements in the Declaration are the following:

> We Indigenous Peoples are sons and daughters of Mother Earth [. . .] We have lived in coexistence with her for thousands of years, with our wisdom and cosmic spirituality linked to nature. [. . .] The aggression towards Mother Earth and the repeated assaults and violations against our soils, air, forests, rivers, lakes, biodiversity, and the cosmos are assaults against us. Before, we used to ask permission for

everything. Now, coming from developed countries, it is pre-
sumed that Mother Earth must ask us for permission.[2]

Agrarian activism, meanwhile, has to be understood in the
context of the ongoing crisis faced by so many of the world's
roughly 1.5 billion smallholding farmers. While the preceding
chapters have covered some of the larger-scale and higher-
profile aspects of this crisis, there are also quieter, but perhaps
even more important, processes at work. These involve not
the hard-to-miss processes of mass dispossession, regulatory change and state territorial control (though they can be
related to them), but the day-to-day difficulties of making
a living as a farmer in the South. How do you make ends
meet, for instance, when the costs of key inputs for farming
– seeds, petrol, fertilizer, capital – are both volatile and often
high? When large-scale, well-financed and politically better
connected agribusinesses (in your own country and abroad),
and even your own wealthier, harder-working, savvier and/
or luckier neighbours can out-compete you in the market-
place? When governments in northern countries subsidize
their agricultural sectors and protect national markets against
key southern crops like cotton, sugar and rice? When a bad
season, or an illness, or the wedding of a child, can plunge
you hopelessly into debt? And, perhaps most profoundly,
when you know that your children have no interest in becoming farmers; that they are not acquiring the skills required for
agricultural work, and hope to move to the city?

To some, the long-term, grinding pressures which lead
people to succumb to debt, to lose their land or to fail to pass it
on to the next generation, and to leave farming, represent an
inevitable and, ultimately, welcome process of rising productivity in agriculture. As better capitalized farmers, using more
modern techniques, seeds and inputs, produce more food per
hectare of land and hour of labour, it becomes possible to feed

the world with fewer people working as farmers. This, in turn, allows former farmers to escape from the poverty that is the lot of most smallholders and take up (or at least see their children take up) higher-paying and less back-breaking jobs in the industrial or service sectors. This need not imply a move to the city: across much of the South, even people in rural areas are shifting their livelihood activities away from farming. The vision is that ultimately the whole world will come to resemble North America, Western Europe, and parts of North-East Asia, with very high levels of urbanization and only 2–3 per cent of the population engaged in agriculture. Indeed, for many, this process of 'agrarian transition' – from a poor society dominated by agriculture to a rich one dominated by industry and services – is more or less the definition of economic development.

Even advocates of this point of view acknowledge that the process of 'transition' is intensely painful for the people going through it. Efforts to deal with some of the problems that face smallholding farmers, together with resistance to the more high-profile problems noted above, have been central to the rising contention around rural land across much of the South since the 1990s. These mobilizations are not just about land for agriculture; as *Powers of Exclusion* put it, they involve 'popular mobilizations under a range of banners (those of the poor, the citizen, the political party, the peasant, the ethnic or indigenous group) for access to land as a productive resource, as a backstop for precarious livelihoods, and as a symbol of identity and belonging'. The scale of what is happening also varies widely – from transnational NGOs working on agricultural issues, to national movements of peasants and the landless, to regional struggles over the impacts of dams and the expansion of particular cities, to tiny neighbourhood groups protesting the enclosure of a sliver of collectively held land. Increasingly, however, mobilizations around land are transnational in the sense we have used throughout the book. Finally, this discussion of mobilization and activism should not obscure the fact that people do not necessarily object to changes in their land relations. This book has already shown that some rural people have been willing to see their land acquired by states or businesses, to welcome expanded government authority over their lives and to adapt to new regulations around titling and conservation if they see some benefit for themselves. People may seek to engage with these processes on their own terms, and we cannot assume 'resistance' as the natural response.

Transnational indigenous and agrarian movements

Transnational activism around indigenous and agrarian issues has expanded at the same time as, and in interaction with, transnational mobilizing around other issues. There are at least four reasons for this broad trend. First and perhaps most straightforwardly, the falling price of air transportation, along with access to new communications technology like fax machines, email, the internet and Skype, have made it much easier for activists to keep in touch, share information and travel internationally. Second, globalization, and especially expanding flows of international trade and investment and the intensification of transboundary environmental problems, have meant that the threats and difficulties people face increasingly originate outside their own country. Transnational problems have encouraged people to pitch some of their activism above the level of the state. Third, it is not only threats that have become transnational or (in some cases) global, but also opportunities. As some policy-making has shifted from the national to the international level, whether through fora where states gather to negotiate (such as the World Trade Organization and the UN General Assembly) or through the expanding sway of international organizations with some independent capacity for decision-making and action (like the International Monetary Fund and the World Bank), so activists have had more incentive to focus on the international level. Relatedly, activists (especially in the South) have found that, when their domestic struggles are not bearing fruit, they can mobilize transnational allies (other activists, states or international organizations) to pressure their own government. Margaret Keck and Kathryn Sikkink label this tactic the 'boomerang' effect.[3]

The fourth reason that transnational activism has grown is that states, donor agencies and international organizations have encouraged it to. While we usually think of activists as having a contentious and oppositional relationship to power, states, donors and international organizations in fact often work closely with transnational networks and NGOs. They rely on them for information, and they hire them to do consulting and development work. More broadly, norm shifts that took place in international politics in the 1980s and early 1990s mean that states are now expected to consult with and ensure the 'participation' of civil society groups in making international policy. 'Stakeholders' must now be engaged with if the outcomes of policy debates are to be seen as legitimate. One consequence is that donors have been willing, and at times eager, to fund the activities of activists (especially those based in the South) and their participation in international conferences. This dynamic exists between activists as well, as northern NGOs have been keen to pursue partnerships with groups from the South and have provided funds to support them.

Transnational indigenous and agrarian activism also share some other dynamics. One example is the interaction of NGOs and networks that seek directly to represent indigenous people and peasants with those that do research and advocacy work in those areas but whose memberships are mostly not composed of the people they seek to support. This combination can be a productive one, but relationships between often better funded, middle-class, northern NGOs and movements that try to represent people who are largely quite poor can also lead to tensions. These can be exacerbated when the latter are at some level financially dependent upon, and perhaps even in competition for funding from, the former. A second important point to note is the dual nature of most transnational movements, which try to speak and act with a unified voice while being made up of a large number of diverse groups from a range of countries. Such networks are both actors and arenas of interaction. A third point is that activism is not primarily transnational. Activists also work in pursuit of their goals at the local, sub-national, national and regional scales, and transnational networks are by their nature mostly a venue for such groups to work on shared goals.

Transnational indigenous movements

The 1970s were a period of rapid expansion of indigenous activism in the Americas in particular, and saw the creation of key transnational indigenous networks (such as the Inuit Circumpolar Conference discussed in chapter 3) [4] It was also in the mid-1970s that indigenous activists began to take part in the UN system. This participation involved both the use by activists of UN human rights committees to monitor and pressure their home states, and increasingly formal participation (including by the Global Indigenous Peoples' Caucus) in the epic negotiations around what would become the Declaration on the Rights of Indigenous Peoples. Since the establishment of the UN Permanent Forum on Indigenous Issues in 2002, indigenous groups have been the only non-state actors to have an explicit and formal right to vote in a UN body. After a long struggle, indigenous peoples have gained recognition in the UN system *as* peoples, rather than as 'populations' or as 'indigenous persons'. This recognition carries with it certain rights to self-determination that are codified in UNDRIP. The definition of 'indigenous', however, is a complex and contested question on which UNDRIP does not take a clear position, and one on which different states have different opinions. Countries like China, India and Indonesia have denied that the concept has any relevance within their borders.

Land issues have been at the heart of transnational indigenous activism. The key international documents that have resulted from this transnational activism, most notably the International Labour Organization's Convention No. 169 (the Indigenous and Tribal Peoples Convention) and UNDRIP, lay out far-reaching rights of indigenous peoples to land, rights that we can understand in this book's terms as having profound implications for land as territory, land as property and the way in which land is regulated. ILO 169 was approved by the ILO's General Assembly in 1989 and came into force in 1991, and as of late 2011 had been ratified by 22 countries, most of them in Latin America. Unlike UNDRIP, which is a Declaration, this Convention is legally binding on states that have ratified it. Key land-related elements of ILO 169 appear in Article 14.1, which specifies that 'The rights of ownership and possession of the peoples concerned over the lands which they traditionally occupy shall be recognized', and in 15.1, which states that 'the rights of the peoples concerned to the natural resources pertaining to their lands shall be specially safeguarded. These rights include the rights of these peoples to participate in the use, management, and conservation of these resources.' Article 15.2 goes on to lay out the right of indigenous and tribal peoples to be consulted with regard to the use of their land's sub-surface resources in cases in which the state retains ownership of them, although, as critics have pointed out, this right to consultation does not include a right to veto.

While ILO 169 laid out an extensive range of indigenous and tribal rights around land, UNDRIP goes further. Perhaps most notably, it recognizes the right of indigenous peoples, like other peoples in world politics, to self-determination. This right should not be interpreted to mean that indigenous peoples have the right to secede from their own states. UNDRIP assumes that indigenous rights exist within the framework of a state that is not itself indigenous. As Cree leader Ted Moses put it in regard to the draft UNDRIP in 2003, 'The Crees have no interest in secession from Canada. We want self-determination to be recognised so that we can finally become part of Canada.'[5] One of the ways in which the right to self-determination takes UNDRIP further than ILO 169 is that states are now obliged to obtain the 'free and informed consent' of indigenous peoples 'prior to the approval of any project affecting their lands or territories and other resources, particularly in connection with the development, utilization or exploitation of mineral, water or other resources' (Article 32.2).

These and other international instruments recognize indigenous rights to land as territory and property, and to participation in regulating and controlling the use of their land, that go much further than those available to other minority groups recognized in the UN system. While the proof of these declarations, conventions and agreements is, of course, in the implementation, there are indications that even the non-binding UNDRIP is having a substantial impact on policy frameworks in some areas. The World Bank and other development agencies, for instance, have worked to incorporate even 'soft law' declarations of indigenous rights into their operational policies. One of the most interesting areas where indigenous rights instruments are having an effect is in the

Latin American countries that have ratified ILO 169. These countries are witnessing the emergence of a highly complex jurisprudence around indigenous land rights that ties together ILO 169, UNDRIP, international human rights instruments at the inter-American level, and national laws (including references to the national laws and jurisprudence of other states).[6] This jurisprudence is grappling with and ruling on some of the tensions and uncertainties that characterize land-rights recognition, including questions of the demarcation, delimiting and formalization of indigenous claims, the competing rights of non-indigenous peoples who have legally come into possession of what is recognized as indigenous land, and requirements to undertake environmental and social impact assessments in relation to development projects.

Transnational agrarian movements

Although transnational agrarian movements have a long history, they emerged as notable actors on the contemporary international scene later than did indigenous movements.[7] Since the early 1990s, however, a diverse set of groups and networks has been engaging in transnational agrarian activism. Land issues have not, until relatively recently, been a major focus of this work, which has dealt more with issues like trade and intellectual property rights. It is also important to note that transnational agrarian activists mobilize around land in a context in which there is no internationally recognized general right to land (in the sense that there is, say, a right to food). The UN Universal Declaration of Human Rights does recognize a right to housing, and Article 17 lays out the right to own property (both alone and in association with others) and not to be arbitrarily deprived of it. Some countries (such as South Africa) do recognize some form of general right to land at the national level.

One important group that seeks to represent farmers'

interests internationally is the International Federation of Agricultural Producers, which was founded in 1946. A younger, more radical, and, by now, more prominent group is La Vía Campesina, which was launched in 1993. As of mid-2012, Vía Campesina claimed to bring together roughly 150 local and national organizations representing 'millions of peasants, small and medium-sized farmers, landless people, women farmers, indigenous people, and agricultural workers' from 70 countries. Vía Campesina's representation is strongest in the Americas and Western Europe (where it had its origins), South and South-East Asia, and parts of Africa; the group's website does not list any members from China, the Middle East or the former Soviet Union. The movement has turned its attention to a wide range of international actors and fora, but it draws a distinction between international financial institutions such as the World Bank and the IMF (with which it will not work) and groups within the UN system, such as the FAO and the IFAD, with which it has been willing to engage. There are also transnational networks that incorporate researchers and activists who are not themselves farmers, including the Food First International Action Network (FIAN) and the Land Research Action Network (LRAN). Two other important networks for transnational agrarian activism are the International Land Coalition, an alliance of non-state groups and international organizations (including the World Bank) that works on land access issues, and the International Planning Committee for Food Sovereignty.

With respect to land specifically, we can note three major strands of transnational activism. The first of these is the Global Campaign for Agrarian Reform that Vía Campesina and its allies have waged since 1999.[8] This campaign has opposed the 'market-led agrarian reform' (MLAR) that the World Bank and other international and bilateral development agencies have promoted since the 1990s and that was often closely tied up with the international land titling projects discussed in chapter 4. Proponents of MLAR sought to return land reform to the policy agenda without repeating what they saw as the mistakes of classic post-war forms of land redistribution. While earlier approaches, they argued, had been top-down, state-driven, confrontational and confiscatory (in that they were designed around the expropriation of land from large-scale landholders, usually with compensation, and its redistribution to the landless and land-poor), MLAR sought to put the market to work in redistributing land. The core idea was that funds would be provided to the landless and land-poor to enable them to purchase land from landlords at market prices through 'willing buyer, willing seller' transactions. This approach was meant to deal with inequalities in land ownership while also ensuring, through the market logic described in chapter 5, that land would end up in the hands of those able to use it most productively.

Reaction to MLAR among farmers was mixed, and not all rural people and organizations opposed it. Vía Campesina, however, rejected MLAR as a neoliberal project. The strategies that the movement adopted against MLAR reflect the ways that agrarian reform had become, by the early 2000s, a more transnational affair than it had been in the 'classic' reform period of the early Cold War. With international financial institutions and bilateral development agencies key actors in MLAR's promotion, Vía Campesina followed the logic expressed at the beginning of this section by taking its campaign to the transnational level. This move is visible both in the alliances that Vía Campesina developed with FIAN and LRAN around this issue, and also in the clear international target that the World Bank presented to the campaign. While Saturnino M. Borras Jr argues that the Global Campaign for Agrarian Reform has had some impact, through its opposition to market-led agrarian reform, on the framing of debates around international land policy, he sees very limited reform in the more substantive areas of actual policy, procedure and behaviour.

A second Vía Campesina project with a significant land component is the campaign for a UN declaration of peasants' rights.[9] Transnational peasant groups began to engage with the UN system in the late 1990s. From around 2000, Vía Campesina began a push for recognition of peasants' rights at the UN that was clearly modelled on the contemporaneous campaign for UNDRIP. A draft of the proposed Declaration was produced in 2002, with a revision following in 2009. Both drafts combined rights that were already in existence within the UN system with new ones. The rights claimed for 'peasants (women and men)' under the heading of what Article IV of the 2009 draft calls 'Right to Land and Territory' include the right to own land collectively or individually for housing and farming, to 'toil' on the land, to manage water resources, to security of tenure and 'to reject all kinds of land acquisition and conversion for economic purpose', and to benefit from land reform. Article IV.11 also refers to 'the right to agricultural land that can be irrigated to ensure food sovereignty for growing population [sic]', which implies that the state should be obliged to provide irrigable land to peasants.

Vía Campesina has had some success in gaining a hearing for the idea of a declaration at the UN, and indeed the movement's coordinator, Henry Saragih, spoke to the draft before the UN General Assembly in 2009. As Marc Edelman and Carwil James have pointed out, however, acceptance of the draft declaration in anything like its current form would represent a major transformation in the UN human rights framework. Prospects for the draft's adoption are slim to nil. Interestingly, one way in which the draft seeks to make its case is by engaging in the 'culturalization' of peasants: as Edelman and James put it, 'In effect, peasants are represented not only as "rights holders", but as the same kind of culture-possessing population that indigenous people are recognized to be within the indigenous rights regime.'[10] Such a framing suggests that they are not just people with property but also, as the heading above states, groups with territory.

Finally, transnational groups and networks concerned with agrarian issues have been galvanized into action by the global land grab. Activism on this issue started slightly before the beginning of the land grab debate proper. The food price crisis of 2007–8 sparked a surge of concern over the extent to which agricultural production worldwide was being diverted away from food uses and towards biofuels, and land issues were very much a part of the critique. It was the late 2008 GRAIN report discussed in chapter 4, however, that put the issue into the public eye under the 'land grab' heading. From the perspective of the social movement literature, the land grab is exactly the kind of issue that should lead to intense transnational activism. The issue's 'framing', which described powerful foreign actors joining forces with corrupt state officials to kick small-scale farmers in some of the world's poorest countries off their land, made these projects look straightforwardly appalling and invoked obvious parallels with colonialism. A wide range of transnational groups, including Vía Campesina, FIAN, and the International Institute for Environment and Development, have thrown themselves into the anti-land grab campaign. Within the UN system, Olivier de Schutter, the UN Special Rapporteur for the Right to Food, has taken a strong position against land-grabbing. As we saw in chapter 4, even the World Bank has raised concerns about 'large-scale land acquisitions', at least on the policy side; at the same time, actual World Bank projects and funding through the International Finance Corporation continue to support the opening up of land to investment.

While powerful international actors have not ignored activism around the land grab, they have responded not by trying to prevent 'large-scale land acquisitions' but rather by trying to create a policy framework that will make them more acceptable. One example is the effort to create an international 'code of conduct' that aims at the win–win–win outcomes discussed in chapter 4. The FAO, IFAD, UNCTAD and the World Bank have developed seven 'Principles for Responsible Agricultural Investment that Respects Rights, Livelihoods and Resources'. The principles are: respecting land and resource rights; ensuring food security; transparency and good governance; consultation and participation; responsible agro-enterprise investing; social sustainability; and environmental sustainability. Critics argue that this approach tries to put lipstick on a pig. A potentially more positive development was the May 2012 FAO endorsement of the *Voluntary Guidelines on the Responsible Governance of Tenure of Land, Fisheries and Forests in the Context of National Food Security* negotiated (with civil society participation, including from Vía Campesina) at the CFS.

Urbanization, dispossession and rightful resistance at China's rural–urban fringe

China's economic growth over the last three decades (and more) has been extraordinary. Between 1980 and 2010, China's gross domestic product (GDP) grew at an average rate of 10 per cent per year, and per capita GDP (measured in constant 2000 US dollars) increased thirteen-fold from US$186 to US$2,423. Over the same period, the percentage of the population living in cities rose from 20 to 45 per cent (still well below the world average). Put another way, over those thirty years China's urban population increased by 400 million people – by far the most spectacular urban expansion in a single country in human history.[11] In the 1980s especially, living standards in the Chinese countryside (which is still home to one third of

the world's farming families) shot up as agriculture was dec-
ollectivized and market opportunities reappeared. Increases
in agricultural productivity meant that very large numbers of
people were, depending on how you look at it, either 'freed' or
'ejected' from farming, and many of them moved to the cities
in search of jobs in the industrial or service sectors. China has
not, however, repealed the Mao-era *hukou* system of residency
registration which restricts people's access to legal work and
social services outside the locale where they are registered. As a
result, huge numbers of people in China are essentially illegal
immigrants in their own country. One estimate for the early
2000s put the 'floating population' of illegal migrant labour in
the cities at something like 150 million people.

With GDP, urban population and industrial production skyrocketing, and with the Chinese political economy
becoming more dominated by cities and urban state-owned
corporations after the 1980s, there has been a massive drive
to redevelop land in existing urban cores and to expand urban
areas both administratively and in terms of land use. Old
urban neighbourhoods have been transformed into core business districts filled with spectacular skyscrapers and high-end
real estate, while, on the rural–urban fringe, there has been
a push for the kinds of peri-urban land uses discussed in the
Indian context in chapter 4. In the 1990s, land was in high
demand for industrial parks (*kaifaqu*), which were relatively
small but extremely numerous. Since around 2000, the cutting edge of urban expansion has been 'new cities' (*xincheng*),
which are much larger (usually in the tens of square kilometres) and are meant to include mixed housing, commercial
and leisure development. While statistics on the amount of
land taken over for these purposes must be treated with cau-
tion, the estimates are breathtaking. One figure suggests that,
between 1987 and 2003, 10–12 million hectares of farmland
(or around 10 per cent of China's arable land) were converted

to non-agricultural uses; another states that, by 2003, 3.6 million hectares had been designated for development zones. As noted above, between 50 and 66 million peasants lost some or all of their land to governmental expropriation for development projects between 1990 and 2002.

Understanding the politics of state land acquisition and dispossession requires some background knowledge of how land is governed in China.[12] According to the Constitution of the People's Republic of China, the state has the final claim over all land. Land is also, however, divided between urban land, which belongs to state agencies, and rural land, which belongs to village collectives which are not themselves part of the state. In 1988, changes were made to the land laws which allowed urban land to be leased for profit (but not sold), but village land may not be so leased. It is possible, however, for village land to become urban land (and thus available for lease), as 'the state' (including urban governments) can requisition any land when doing so is deemed to be in the public interest. Further, since the early 1980s, provincial governments have been converting rural administrative areas into urban ones by upgrading their territorial status or merging them with existing cities. This process has meant that urban jurisdictions have come to control, and to be able to lease out, large areas of what in use terms is rural land. In China's rapidly expanding urban areas, the local state is both the main regulator of land use and the central participant in land development. You-Tien Hsing argues that 'Land-centered accumulation has [. . .] become the main aspiration, the tacit and explicit mandate, and the key strategy behind local state building' in China's cities in a context in which 'local state leaders aspire to be landowners, planners, financiers, and builders, all at the same time.'

Chinese land law is vague about some critical aspects of precisely which branches of the state have authority over which land. While there is not space here to go into the details, the key point is that different types of state agencies are competing for control (both in the sense of administrative jurisdiction and of ownership) over China's land and the enormous amounts of money that can be made from it. Higher-level urban governments at the municipal and district level, for instance, compete with governments at the township and village levels for control over rural land held by village collectives. The *kaifaqu* of the 1990s were primarily the creations of lower-level governments, but the much larger *xincheng* of the 2000s are projects of higher-level urban governments. Precisely who has authority over what in these struggles is not always clear, but it *is* clear that much of what goes on at the local level is straightforwardly illegal. Township leaders, in particular, have illegally leased or approved the conversions of vast amounts of village land. The central government's own Ministry of Land and Resources reported that there were 131,000 illegal land seizures involving 100,000 hectares of land in 2006 alone, while between 2000 and 2007 14,000 Communist Party cadres were either issued warnings or investigated over land issues.[13] One of the most important features of land struggles in China is the enormous difficulty that the central state has in monitoring and controlling the activities of lower levels of government and the ability of local officials to seize land for their own gain. Indeed, the rural-urban fringe in China is in some respects reminiscent of the 'frontier' areas discussed in chapter 3. Officials who are part of the 'state', but have dramatically different priorities to those enshrined in central policy and operate in what Hsing calls a state land tenure 'gray zone', have rushed to grab land from rural people before other state agencies can take control of it themselves.

Chinese peasants (*nongmin*) living relatively close to an urban centre, then, are likely to be confronted with state agencies looking to seize their land in a context of ultimate state land ownership, unclear land law and a competitive dynamic in which a state agency that waits too long to act may see the plum grabbed by someone else. These, however, are far from the only pressures Chinese peasants face. Corrupt and venal local officials pose a variety of problems beyond trying to seize land, including levying illegal and extremely high taxes and service fees. Pollution in many parts of China is bad enough to be a threat to both human health and agriculture. The Chinese political economy is also now characterized by extremely high levels of inequality between urban and rural areas, between the relatively wealthy coast and the desperately poor interior, and between the well-connected and everybody else. The plight of China's peasants, and in particular the pressures they face from local-level government officials, has been laid out in a series of reports on specific villages in Anhui Province in a 2004 book by Chen Guidi and Wu Chuntao translated into English as *Will the Boat Sink the Water? The Life of China's Peasants*.

How have China's peasants reacted to this pressure, and to land seizures in particular? China's Public Security Ministry keeps annual statistics on what it calls 'public order disturbances'. According to these figures, 2005 saw 87,000 cases of such 'disturbances', 40–50 per cent of which took place in the countryside.[14] While the main targets of peasant protest in the 1990s were high taxes and corrupt local officials, by the 2000s land seizures and forced evictions emerged as the key concerns. There has been an enormous upsurge of contention around land in a China that is clearly not entirely the cowed, stable society it is often assumed to be in the West.

While China is thus no stranger to contentious politics, these 'incidents' have largely shared two characteristics that have made them less offensive to the central government than they would otherwise have been. First, they have primarily been quite localized, taking place at the level of the village or town rather than the province or country, and connections between them have been fairly limited. Second, they have largely sought not to challenge the authority of the state, but rather to invoke, affirm and appeal to it. Kevin O'Brien and Lianjiang Li describe the characteristic form of contemporary Chinese contentious politics as 'rightful resistance'. This form of protest involves confronting local officials with the gap between their actions and the central state policies, laws, regulations and priorities that they are meant to be following and implementing. Protesters may, for instance, draw attention to laws limiting the amount of tax that peasants are to pay, or to regulations regarding the conversion of agricultural land, or even to less formal and broader government priorities such as reducing the 'burdens' on the peasantry. Rightful resistance thus involves 'a contention based on strict adherence to established values'. Tactics can range from pointing out the law to officials in the course of their business, to court proceedings and petitions to higher-level authorities, to demonstrations and occupations of land slated for expropriation and clearance. Peasant efforts to make their oppression at the hands of township officials known at the county, provincial or national level are a constant feature of the protest stories narrated by Chen and Wu in *Will the Boat Sink the Water?*

Local government officials are rarely thrilled to have their alleged crimes pointed out, whether to villagers, to themselves or (especially) to their superiors. One county-level official interviewed by O'Brien and Li gave a local-state perspective on rightful resistance by saying that 'As soon as ordinary people learn anything about the law they become impossible to govern.'[15] Some officials respond to challenges with stonewalling or with promises of investigation and amelioration that never materialize. Others do not recognize the rights of villagers to complain and may pursue protest 'ringleaders' with trumped-up legal actions, police harassment and violence.

When rightful resistance is expressed through demonstrations and land occupations, local officials have responded by mobilizing the police, thugs and criminal organizations to break them up by force, with protesters ending up in jail, injured or dead. One strategy employed by some local governments has been the mobilization, on the day that demolition on seized land is due to start, of not just public and private forces (police and thugs) but of hundreds of regular government employees, such as teachers. Such campaigns, however, can be difficult to sustain. Hsing writes that 'For local cadres responsible for carrying out demolition and forced relocation, the job could be as tense as warfare – and wars are costly, financially and politically.'[16] Compromise and compensation, rather than confrontation, can emerge as a more appealing strategy, especially given the enormous sums officials stand to gain when the land acquisition process is complete.

The 'rightful resistance' strategy assumes that the state is not a unitary organization. Protesters put their faith (whether genuinely or tactically) in central state policies and laws meant to protect peasants from predation, hope that local officials will be concerned about the prospect of punishment from the centre and seek alliances with higher-level officials who have their own reasons for supporting them. Central government figures can be surprisingly receptive to peasant protest. Trying to align the behaviour of local-level governments with central priorities and to keep a lid on local-level official corruption and oppression is, again, one of the top goals of the Chinese leadership. Since the early 2000s, too, the government has prioritized a range of large-scale policy measures to try to deal with pressures on agriculture, rural areas and the peasantry. These have included the 2006 removal of taxes on agriculture and efforts to restrain land grabs, including a 2004 freeze on the conversion of agricultural land. Central leaders worry, however, that their campaigns to bring local officials into line tend to end up being (in the words of two state officials) 'hot in the center, warm in the provinces, lukewarm in the cities, cool in the counties, cold in the townships, and frozen in the villages'.[17] Peasant protest can indicate to central officials where there are problems that need to be dealt with. This does not mean that the centre will always support peasant protest; very often, higher-level officials side with local governments or try to sweep problems under the carpet. Certainly there is very little room either for criticism of the Chinese Communist Party or for high levels of coordination between movements in different parts of the country.

While rightful resistance is a widespread and fascinating aspect of peasant protest in China, peasants also respond to the pressures they are under, and especially to land seizures, in ways that might be seen as falling on either side of it. Some more transgressive protests go beyond rightful resistance in their scale and use of violence. Some protests have swelled to thousands, if not tens of thousands, of people, and have been responded to with paramilitary force. Government estimates that 8,200 township and county officials were injured or killed in 1993 suggest the level of peasant anger and, again, of the frontier-like conditions of some local Chinese governance. When protesters turn to property damage, arson and violence against persons, it becomes very difficult for them to frame their actions as supportive of the political authority and priorities of the Communist Party, even when they continue to appeal to central policy priorities.

Land seizures and evictions, however, do not always result in protest and resistance. Far from it. Peasants may feel too intimidated to object or may feel that their prospects of getting a positive hearing from higher-level officials are too low. Very often, villages split over reactions to land seizures, with some peasants deciding to accept compensation payments and new land and housing (or promises of those things) and move on, while others try to stick it out. Officials encourage such splits by cutting deals with village leaders for their support. Resistance is difficult in the absence of village solidarity and, as evictions, demolitions, and land clearance begin, services are cut off and harassment increases, most people will give in. Those who hold out are referred to as 'nail households' – isolated homes without electricity or water in the midst of construction sites and piles of garbage.

While peasant acquiescence to land seizures may look like defeat, this is not always true. Hsing argues that some village collectives have been able to do quite well out of land conversion, and indeed to strengthen their collective institutions, by bargaining and allying with officials and using what leverage they have to ensure that they maintain access to at least some collective village land as it rapidly rises in value. This pattern is quite similar to that analysed by Michael Levien in Jaipur, where opposition to a development zone was reduced by giving (some) people land in the zone, and hence a stake in it. Even for people who are not so fortunate, Hsing indicates that conversion can still look like the best option in a bad situation:

> In many cases, especially in more industrialized and commercialized areas and for the younger generation, peasants are not opposed to conversion of farmland, as long as they are fairly compensated. In the rural fringe, where peasants are caught between low returns from staple agriculture and a shortage of non-farm jobs, the promise of a sizeable amount of cash for land is extremely alluring. Promised compensation can bring new hope to dead-end rural lives.[18]

Conclusion

Three main points about activism around land emerge from this chapter. First, activism takes place at a variety of spatial scales. Some of the groups discussed above are organized at the scale of the village; others have memberships that span the globe. Groups organized at one scale can, of course, try to make their influence felt at another. Chinese villagers travel to Beijing to put their case to the central government; national indigenous groups pressure UN human rights committees to intervene in the politics of their home country; transnational NGOs working on agricultural issues oppose land grabs that may be backed by powerful local actors. Much of the most important mobilization continues to take place locally and nationally, and few 'boomerangs' are being thrown out into international politics from China's urban–rural fringe. There has, however, been a clear shift over the last two decades towards pitching more activism around land at the transnational level, notably through efforts to engage with and mobilize against organizations like the UN, the World Bank, the FAO and the regional development banks. This is taking place in part because electronic communications technologies, cheaper international air travel and the interest of northern groups (states, international organizations and NGOs) in funding collaboration with partners in the South have contributed to an upsurge in activist work across borders. But it is also a result of the ways international organizations have sought to take a larger role in the formation of policy around land – the World Bank through its promotion of market-led agrarian reform and liberalized investment in land, the UN through its work on indigenous land rights, the FAO through its concerns over agricultural development. Activism around land is shifting to the transnational level in part because policy-making around land is increasingly carried out there.

Second, activism is directed at land's role as territory, its function as property and the ways in which land use and possession are regulated. The rights for which indigenous activists have fought at the UN make this point very clearly.

Indigenous peoples have demanded to be recognized precisely as peoples and thus as having territories of their own over which they hold collective authority. They have fought for assurances that their property will not be arbitrarily seized from them. And they have been able to enshrine, in UNDRIP, the state's obligation to seek their free, prior and informed consent before any development projects involving their land are undertaken. This combination of territorial, property-based and regulatory activism is also visible in many of the Chinese villages that are having their land expropriated for urban development. Villagers do not simply try to defend what they see as their property; their 'rightful resistance' appeals to regulations regarding the proper procedures for converting agricultural to urban land, and they invoke their membership in village collectives to make a more territorial case for their rights to the land.

Third, the upsurge in activism described in this chapter has been driven at all scales by the pressures that small-scale farmers and indigenous peoples face around land. Some of these, most obviously land seizures (for agribusiness projects, for industry, for urban expansion, for conservation zones), are high-profile and come with easily identifiable villains. Others are more long-term, more insidious and structural; they relate to the declining ability of smallholding farmers to live under conditions that are highly competitive and that more often than not are rigged against them. These pressures have had complex and contradictory impacts on agrarian activism. They increase the incentive to mobilize, but they also make that mobilization more difficult, both by making life harder and, more profoundly, by changing rural people's attitudes towards land. As people search for livelihood opportunities outside of the agricultural sector that hold out more promise than the physically demanding, risky and unremunerative work of farming, land may come to occupy a different – though not necessarily less important – position in their lives and identities. The consequences of these changes will not all point in the same direction. It is worth ending the chapter, however, with Marc Edelman's 2008 take on some of the potential implications for activism:

> the *campesino* of today is usually not the *campesino* of even 15 years ago. The individual who farms during the rainy season, works on urban construction sites during the dry season, rents out his pickup and provides mechanic services to neighbours, sells imported Chinese toys and pirated CDs in town on weekends, and receives a monthly wire of 50 dollars from a son living in New York is less likely to fully identify with the agenda of the historic *campesino* organizations than was his more fully 'peasantized' parent or grandparent.[19]

CHAPTER SEVEN

Conclusion

Apriantono's saga

In 2005, the Indonesian government announced plans to establish what the country's Minister of Agriculture Anton Apriantono said would be 'the world's largest integrated oil palm plantation' on 1.8 million hectares of land along the border between the provinces of West and East Kalimantan and the Malaysian states of Sarawak and Sabah.[1] This astonishing project, which built on pre-existing initiatives along the border, would have developed a continuous corridor of monocultured oil palm stretching from one side of the huge island of Borneo to the other. It was also being planned in conjunction with a 2,000-km road along the border and the expansion of the military's presence in the area. The 'corridor' scheme, however, has not come to fruition. While plenty of oil palm development has taken place on the border, the grand plan for a continuous plantation was undermined in part by the fact that little of the land in question was actually suitable for growing oil palm, and in part by the strong opposition it faced from a range of sources. Why did the government launch this ill-conceived project, and why did the plan fail? The answers to these questions draw together the core themes of this book. They highlight the value of the interlinked concepts of territory, regulation and property in the analysis of land, point to many of the central empirical topics of the preceding chapters and emphasize the importance of transnational dynamics in land politics.

An analysis of the government's concerns about the area can begin with territory. The relatively sparsely populated and inaccessible areas of West and East Kalimantan along the border with Malaysia are frontiers or, more specifically, borderlands, and have for decades been 'a source of extreme anxiety for the modern Indonesian state that views the border population as unreliable and potentially subversive subjects'.[2] The Iban and other ethnic groups who live in the area share ethnic ties with the majority population in Sarawak (as was the case with the Pashtuns living in Afghanistan and Pakistan in chapter 3), and they are economically more integrated into Malaysia than Indonesia. This situation has long led central officials to worry about the level of Indonesian nationalism felt by people in the area. The perceived threats are also external: one government official worried in 2005 that 'there is no clear agreement on the borderline between the two countries and many border poles are damaged or removed', while the minister of agriculture stated that the project was aimed in part at 'strengthening our border against our neighbour Malaysia'. Officials also see the borderlands as a lawless zone characterized by what, from the state's point of view, are criminal activities, including illegal logging, smuggling and illegal border crossings, and by a broader condition of illegibility. The oil palm corridor, the border road and the new military posts were seen as addressing the external and internal sides of the national security and development challenges to what President Yudhoyono called the 'territorial integrity' of Indonesia. Together, they would turn Indonesia's 'backyard' (*halaman belakang*) into its 'front porch' (*halaman depan*). They would do this by providing employment (including to transmigrants from Java), spreading prosperity, improving accessibility and legibility, creating a 'buffer zone' against Malaysian influence and generally increasing the state's presence along the border.

State territorial priorities at the frontier were tied up with worries about regulation and property. On the regulatory side, the central state's influence over land use and allocation had been waning since the fall of the Suharto regime in 1998, and, more specifically, since post-Suharto measures of administrative decentralization had reassigned extensive regulatory powers over land to the district level. Prominent among these reallocated powers was the new ability of districts to assign small forest concessions. The central government was keen to rein this in, but its 2002 revocation of the new concessions was largely ignored. On the property side, the government fretted that large parts of the area were effectively under the control of Malaysian 'gangsters'. The oil palm corridor promised not just to take control of the land out of their hands, but to open up highly profitable logging and plantation opportunities for other interests. Ironically, the main investors the government expected to take part in the project were the Chinese government and companies from Malaysia – the latter being the very country against which the corridor was meant to create a buffer. This case thus highlights again a point made in chapter 3: giving property rights on the frontier to transnational corporations can be seen by central states as strengthening, not weakening, their sovereignty. The army's interest in the area, finally, must be seen against the background of the strip of timber concessions it had held along the border until the fall of Suharto. A major-general, quoted by Michael Eilenberg, asked: 'Why should we [the army] not open up the border area [for oil palm]? The army controls this area. The border area is the sole property of the army.'

Opposition to the project, finally, also fits well into the core themes of the book. The people living in the borderlands, both elites and the broader population, were by and large opposed, not because they were against oil palm as such but because they saw the corridor as a central government move to reassert control over their land. The project's promises of prosperity, development and employment looked to them like a land grab. The plan was also strongly criticized by local, national and international NGOs concerned with land rights issues and conservation. The World Wide Fund for Nature was particularly hostile because of the threat the corridor posed to its 'Heart of Borneo' initiative, a transnational plan for a conservation zone linking Brunei, Indonesia and Malaysia. The plan also faltered because of differences within the Indonesian state. While the Ministry of Agriculture and the military supported the corridor, the Ministries of Forestry and of Environment both opposed it. The project has been further stymied by continued uncertainty over which levels of government have responsibility for what in the borderlands. In sum, this tale of border tension, frontier territorial control, agricultural land grabs, conservation and transnational activism, with its interconnected roles for territory, regulation and property, draws a thread through all of this book's chapters.

Wrapping up

This book has highlighted the central role that transnational dynamics play in contemporary relations around land. Each of the book's five thematic chapters has focused on a key element of these dynamics. States continue to use various strategies to push for control in their territorial 'frontiers', moves which the people who live in those areas respond to in varying ways. Rising corporate demand for land for a wide range of purposes – agriculture, industry, commerce, tourism, resource extraction, infrastructure, speculation – has led transnational actors to engage in widespread interventions across the South in order to take possession of land themselves or to reshape the regulatory frameworks that govern access to it. Intense transnational interest in land formalization

(especially titling) and conservation has prompted interventions with respect to who actually holds rights to land
(property) and to the rules about how they can hold it and what
they may, may not and must do with it (regulation). Activism
around land is also increasingly transnational, a shift especially notable in the activities of transnational indigenous and
agrarian movements. One of the most remarkable trends,
finally, is the fact that little land has been transferred from one
state to another by war since the late 1970s. Given the rising
and multifaceted transnational interest in land documented
in this book, it should not be forgotten that states have largely
eschewed the most traditional way of gaining control over
land: going to war for it. When European states needed land
in the nineteenth century, they went after it in different ways
than they do today. (From the perspective of the people whose
land is being grabbed, however, the differences may not be
obvious.)

While these large-scale transnational trends are vital to
understanding contemporary land relations, much of this
book has been about complexity. I have provided detailed
studies from a number of countries and areas (though even
these have mostly been pitched at a fairly high spatial scale)
in order to emphasize the ways in which 'global' trends can,
in the land relations of any particular place, play themselves
out in unusual ways, fail to occur or be flatly contradicted.
The reasons for this complexity are many. One is that land is
unendingly heterogeneous in terms of its location, characteristics and quality, and of what has been built on it. A hectare of
Siberian tundra, of Mekong Delta rice paddy, and of mid-town
Manhattan condominiums and businesses are so different
that it can be difficult to think of them as the same kind of
resource. Land is also a fundamental component of almost
all human activities and a core part of human identity. There
is a reason the Kevin Costner movie *Waterworld* was such a

disaster: there is not much you can do without land. The reasons we seek to access land, and the connections we have to it, are incredibly diverse. I have tried to bring some order to this diversity by dividing the core aspects of our relationship to land into territory, property and regulation. Each of these concepts, however, is itself extremely complicated. Property, for instance, encompasses an infinite range of possible combinations of rights to use land, to exclude others from it, to manage it and to transfer it.

The power relations around land, too, are highly complex. It is easy to look at the big picture and the high-profile cases and see an inexorable process of states and TNCs seizing control over land. But there are large areas of land that these actors are not in practice interested in, and their plans for control over the land that does concern them can very often go awry (as both Huang's saga and Apriantono's saga have shown). The cost and difficulty of imposing state control in frontier areas leads to accommodations with local actors, and to efforts to look the other way when states would prefer not to know what is going on – even when the people who live on the frontier are jumping up and down trying to get the state's attention. State officials are often unwilling to try to evict people from land because they are afraid of the consequences, and they may turn to compromise or abandon their plans for this reason. Research on the contemporary global 'land grab' shows how many of the schemes of TNCs fall through, perhaps because they are not approved, perhaps because the project turns out not to look profitable on closer inspection, perhaps because of resistance. Titling projects that mobilize millions of dollars and the lessons of decades of international 'best practice' fail to take hold when people feel that engaging with the state over land administration is not in their interests; conservation areas can turn out to be 'paper parks' ignored by the people who live around them. And while transnational activism captures a lot of media attention (in part because its protagonists are more likely to show up at international events, answer email and maintain websites than are activist neighbourhood associations), transnational agrarian movements have not achieved many of their goals. This book has tried to survey some of the key trends in transnational land relations, but it is not a template to be placed on top of local events.

Turning back to these trends, I would like to note in conclusion one of the more interesting (but so far unremarked) commonalities between many of the transnational themes discussed above: the range of ways in which people are now expected to care about what happens to land that is very far away. I, for instance, am supposed to be outraged, as a Canadian living in southern Ontario, that my country's claim to tiny, distant Hans Island is disputed by the perfidious Danes. I am supposed to worry about Pakistan's control over FATA because of the prospect of terrorist attacks on Canada being launched from there, and because the area has been used as a base from which to attack Canadian soldiers in Afghanistan. I am meant to take an interest in the registration of the property rights of people across the South (since I care about development), in land grabs (since I care about human rights and poverty) and about the establishment of conservation zones (since I care about the environment). This concern for distant land is, obviously, far from new. But the diversity and the detail of the commitments that we are now asked to have to faraway land as territory and property, and to the regulation of its use, are surely unprecedented.

Different groups seek to mobilize this duty to care, and the emotional attachments that we feel to land, in pursuit of their own aims. I have already mentioned the acre of rainforest land that came into my possession (if that is the right term) as a result of a conservationist NGO's efforts to combat deforestation. While I was writing this book, I acquired an interest in a second piece of foreign land. When I opened the tube enclosing a bottle of Laphroaig whisky given to me by two friends, I found a small brochure that made an enticing offer: 'Free! Your own square foot of Islay.' I discovered that, by registering at a website[3] and entering my 'unique purchase number', I would be given a lifetime lease on a tiny plot of land on the Laphroaig brewery's grounds on the Scottish island of Islay. My claim was formalized with what the brochure called a 'personalized certificate of ownership', a somewhat confusing usage given that I was only leasing the land. The certificate explained that the brewery does not offer 'heritable ownership or any right to cut peat, farm sheep or extract minerals from the plot', but this seemed a rather brief explanation of the extent of and limits on my property rights; I am not sure, for instance, whether I could put up a tiny weather station on my plot, or buy out the plots of the people around me and build a hotel. The website is clear, however, that the company wants me to visit my plot, plant my national flag in it and claim my annual rent as leaseholder ('a dram of our finest'). I was also encouraged to chat online with the holders of the plots closest to mine and with the 340,000 other Friends of Laphroaig around the world. The brochure puts a poetic spin on the connections I can form by engaging in what we might call a 'small-scale international land acquisition': 'Open a bottle of Laphroaig and you're opening the *hearts of the community*. The people, their lives, their surroundings – you're holding it all *in your hand*. Form a bond with our lives by claiming your plot of our land. Become a *"Friend of Laphroaig"*.' Territory, regulation and property come together here in pursuit of a straightforward goal: getting people to drink more Laphroaig whisky.

Selected Readings

There are huge literatures on some of the themes and concepts covered in this book. These recommended readings provide some points of entry. I have limited repetition of sources already referenced in the footnotes, and have not for the most part provided additional readings for the case studies (FATA, peri-urban India, etc.).

Chapter 1 focuses on the concepts of territory, regulation, property and land. The concept of territory is covered in David Delaney, *Territory: A Short Introduction* (Malden: Blackwell, 2005). On the regulation of land use, see *Powers of Exclusion: Land Dilemmas in Southeast Asia* (Singapore and Honolulu: NUS Press and University of Hawai'i Press, 2011), by Derek Hall, Philip Hirsch and Tania Murray Li. *Powers of Exclusion* also takes up the question of how people are excluded from land through the powers of regulation, legitimation, the market and force, and surveys the operation of these powers in contemporary South-East Asia. Theoretical treatments of property can be found in Edella Schlager and Elinor Ostrom, 'Property-Rights Regimes and Natural Resources: A Conceptual Analysis', *Land Economics* 68(3) (1992): 249–62, and Franz von Benda-Beckmann, Keebet von Benda-Beckmann and Melanie G. Wiber, 'The Properties of Property', in their edited book *Changing Properties of Property* (New York and Oxford: Berghahn Books, 2006). The relationship between property, authority and access to natural resources (including land) is addressed in the chapters of Thomas Sikor and Christian Lund (eds), *The Politics of Possession: Property, Authority, and Access to Natural Resources* (Malden: Wiley-Blackwell, 2009).

Chapter 2 asked where modern conceptions of state territory and borders came from and how states came to have the territory they have now. On the ways early European colonial powers claimed territory in the Americas, see Patricia Seed, *Ceremonies of Possession: Europe's Conquest of the New World 1492–1640* (Cambridge: Cambridge University Press, 1995). Alexander C. Diener and Joshua Hagen's edited collection *Borderlines and Borderlands: Political Oddities at the Edge of the Nation-State* (London: Rowman & Littlefield, 2010) introduces border-making between states by means of case studies of some of the more peculiar borders in world politics. An accessible introduction to theoretical debates over war and peace can be found in the *Human Security Report 2009/2010: The Causes of Peace and the Shrinking Costs of War* (Human Security Report Project, 2010), Part I, chapters 1 and 2; see also Richard Ned Lebow, *Why Nations Fight: Past and Future Motives for War* (Cambridge: Cambridge University Press, 2010). For arguments about the territorial and property dynamics of specifically capitalist international relations, see Ellen Meiksins Wood, *The Origin of Capitalism: A Longer View* (London and New York: Verso, 2002) and *Empire of Capital* (London and New York: Verso, 2003); and Benno Teschke, *The Myth of 1648: Class, Geopolitics and the Making of Modern International Relations* (London and New York: Verso, 2003).

Frontier dynamics are, as chapter 3 argued, very diverse, and, if one wants to understand these areas, there is no real substitute for reading lots of frontier studies. The following works on South-East Asia all engage with the theoretical literature on frontiers, borderlands and the margins of the state, and would make a great summer of comparative reading: Patricio Abinales, *Making Mindanao: Cotabato and*

Davao in the Formation of the Philippine Nation-State (Manila: Ateneo de Manila University Press, 2000); R. A. Cramb, *Land and Longhouse: Agrarian Transformation in the Uplands of Sarawak* (Copenhagen: NIAS Press, 2007); Rodolphe De Koninck, Stéphane Bernard and Jean-François Bissonnette (eds), *Borneo Transformed: Agricultural Expansion on the Southeast Asian Frontier* (Singapore: NUS Press, 2011); Michael Eilenberg, *At the Edges of States: Dynamics of State Formation in the Indonesian Borderlands* (Leiden: KITLV Press, 2011); Tim Forsyth and Andrew Walker, *Forest Guardians, Forest Destroyers: The Politics of Environmental Knowledge in Northern Thailand* (Seattle: University of Washington Press, 2008); Tania Murray Li, *The Will to Improve: Governmentality, Development, and the Practice of Politics* (Durham, NC: Duke University Press, 2007); John F. McCarthy, *The Fourth Circle: A Political Ecology of Sumatra's Rainforest Frontier* (Stanford: Stanford University Press, 2004); James Scott, *The Art of Not Being Governed: An Anarchist History of Upland Southeast Asia* (New Haven and London: Yale University Press, 2009); Janet Sturgeon, *Border Landscapes: The Politics of Akha Land Use in China and Thailand* (Seattle: University of Washington Press, 2005); Eric Tagliacozzo, *Secret Trades, Porous Borders: Smuggling and States along a Southeast Asian Frontier, 1865– 1915* (New Haven and London: Yale University Press, 2005); Anna Lowenhaupt Tsing, *Friction: An Ethnography of Global Connection* (Princeton: Princeton University Press, 2005); Irina Wenk, 'Land Titling in Perspective: Indigenous–Settler Relations and Territorialization on a Southern Philippine Frontier', in Danilo Geiger (ed.), *Colonization and Conflict: Contemporary Settlement Frontiers in South and Southeast Asia* (Münster: LIT Verlag, forthcoming).

For more on frontiers: the standard source on the state's desire for 'legibility' is James Scott, *Seeing Like a State: How Certain Schemes to Improve the Human Condition have Failed*

(New Haven and London: Yale University Press, 1998).
Catherine Boone's *Political Topographies of the African State:
Territorial Authority and Institutional Choice* (Cambridge:
Cambridge University Press, 2003) seeks to explain why West
African states take different levels of interest in governing
different parts of their territory. Two further sources on the
Canadian Arctic are Ken Coates et al., *Arctic Front: Defending
Canada in the Far North* (Toronto: Thomas Allen Publishers,
2008) and Barry Scott Zellen, *Breaking the Ice: From Land
Claims to Tribal Sovereignty in the Arctic* (Lanham: Lexington
Books, 2008). The novel by Oakley Hall cited in chapter 3 is
Warlock (New York: New York Review Books, 2006 [1958]).

Chapter 4 begins with 'the will to improve', which is discussed in Tania Murray Li's book of the same name cited
above. A very helpful, though somewhat outdated, source on
restrictions on foreign land ownership is Stephen Hodgson,
Cormac Cullinan and Karen Campbell, 'Land Ownership and
Foreigners: A Comparative Analysis of Regulatory Approaches
to the Acquisition and Use of Land by Foreigners', FAO Legal
Papers Online No. 6 (Rome: FAO, 1999). The international
legal framework for foreign investment in natural resources
(including land) is covered in Lorenzo Cotula, *Human Rights,
Natural Resource and Investment Law in a Globalised World:
Shades of Grey in the Shadow of the Law* (London and New
York: Routledge, 2012).

The literature on the 'land grab' is growing rapidly. Three
quite different introductions are Fred Pearce's *The Land
Grabbers: The New Fight over Who Owns the Earth* (Boston:
Beacon Press, 2012); High Level Panel of Experts, 'Land
Tenure and International Investments in Agriculture: A
Report by the High Level Panel of Experts on Food Security
and Nutrition of the Committee on World Food Security'
(Rome: Committee on World Food Security, 2011); and The
World Bank, *Rising Global Interest in Farmland: Can it Yield*

Sustainable and Equitable Benefits? (Washington, DC: The World Bank, 2010). See also the papers by Klaus Deininger, Olivier de Schutter and Tania Murray Li in the forum 'Towards a Better Understanding of Global Land Grabbing', *Journal of Peasant Studies* 38(2) (2011), and, for more detail and case studies, the eighteen papers in the special issue 'The New Enclosures', *Journal of Peasant Studies* 39(3–4) (2012), edited by Ben White et al. The land dynamics of peri-urban South-East Asia are surveyed in Hall, Hirsch and Li, *Powers of Exclusion*. For special economic zones of various kinds in South-East Asia, see Aihwa Ong, 'Graduated Sovereignty in South-East Asia', *Theory, Culture and Society* 17(4) (2000): 55–75. Aravind Adiga's *Last Man in Tower* (London: Atlantic Books, 2011) gives a fictional account of the intimate politics of land conversion in India.

Chapter 5 begins with the linked ideas of improvement, property and conservation in the history of British capitalism and imperialism; on this topic see Richard Drayton, *Nature's Government: Science, Imperial Britain, and the 'Improvement' of the World* (New Haven and London: Yale University Press, 2000). On European efforts to introduce new forms of property rights governance in the colonial world, see Ranajit Guha, *A Rule of Property for Bengal* (Durham and London: Duke University Press, 1996 [1963]); John C. Weaver, *The Great Land Rush and the Making of the Modern World, 1650–1900* (Montreal and Kingston: McGill-Queen's University Press, 2003); and Ellen Meiksins Wood, *Empire of Capital*. Land titling and conservation in South-East Asia since the 1990s, and their impact on people's exclusion from land, are the subjects of chapters 2 and 3 of Hall, Hirsch and Li, *Powers of Exclusion*. De Soto's ideas on land title are presented in *The Mystery of Capital: Why Capitalism Triumphs in the West and Fails Everywhere Else* (New York: Basic Books, 2000); Klaus Deininger's 2003 report *Land Policies for Growth and Poverty Reduction* (Oxford: World

Bank and Oxford University Press, 2003) gives a perspective from the World Bank. A more critical take can be found in the papers in 'Formalisation of Land Rights in the South', a special issue of *Land Use Policy* (26(1) (2009)) edited by Ben Cousins and Espen Sjaastad. The idea that conservation involves 'green grabs' for land and other resources is explored in a special issue of the *Journal of Peasant Studies* (39(2) (2012)) edited by James Fairhead, Melissa Leach and Ian Scoones. The early twenty-first-century relationship between capitalism and conservation is also covered in Dan Brockington, Rosaleen Duffy and Jim Igoe, *Nature Unbound: Conservation, Capitalism and the Future of Protected Areas* (London and Sterling, VA: Earthscan, 2008) and in a 2010 special issue of *Antipode* (42(3)) edited by Brockington and Duffy.

For general background on the discussion of transnational activism in chapter 6, see Margaret E. Keck and Kathryn Sikkink, *Activists Beyond Borders* (Ithaca and London: Cornell University Press, 1998) and Sidney Tarrow, *The New Transnational Activism* (Cambridge: Cambridge University Press, 2005). For more on La Vía Campesina, see their website at viacampesina.org, and Annette Aurélie Desmarais, *La Vía Campesina: Globalization and the Power of Peasants* (Halifax, NS: Fernwood Press, 2007); on transnational agrarian activism more broadly, see Saturnino M. Borras Jr, Marc Edelman and Cristóbal Kay (eds), *Transnational Agrarian Movements Confronting Globalization* (Malden: Wiley-Blackwell, 2008). Wendy Wolford's book *This Land is Ours Now: Social Mobilization and the Meanings of Land in Brazil* (Durham and London: Duke University Press, 2010) gives an ethnographic account of Brazil's Movimento Sem Terra (MST), one of the key social movements in La Vía Campesina. The text of the United Nations Declaration on the Rights of Indigenous Peoples is available at www.un.org/esa/socdev/unpfii/docu ments/DRIPS_en.pdf.

Notes and References

CHAPTER I INTRODUCTION

1 See Andrew Ward and Leslie Hook, 'Chinese tycoon to buy tract of Iceland', *Financial Times*, 29 August 2011, and 'Iceland's president welcomes Chinese interest', *Financial Times*, 2 September 2011; Robert Jackson and Leslie Hook, 'Iceland rejects Chinese investor's land bid', *Financial Times*, 25 November 2011; and 'Tycoon slams Iceland's land sale snub', *Global Times*, 28 November 2011. On the broader question of 'selling Iceland', see Charles Emmerson, *The Future History of the Arctic* (New York: PublicAffairs, 2010), ch. 13.

2 Huang and his supporters in Iceland did not give up. As of mid-2012, it looks like a new version of the deal could be successful, in part because it will see Huang leasing land, rather than buying it, from a shareholding company established by a group of municipalities in the Grímsstaðir area. See Michael Stothard, 'China tycoon may yet gain Iceland foothold', *Financial Times*, 6 March 2012; 'Reykjavik denies approving Chinese tycoon land lease', *Agence France Presse*, 8 May 2012, www.terradaily.com/reports/Reykjavik_denies_approving_Chinese_tycoon_land_lease_999.html (accessed 24 July 2012).

3 My approach has some points of connection with an analytical framework for research on natural resources devised by Christian Lund and Thomas Sikor which emphasizes, among other things, property, authority, access, citizenship and 'territoriality'. See Thomas Sikor and Christian Lund, 'Access and Property: A Question of Politics and Authority', in Thomas Sikor and Christian Lund (eds), *The Politics of Possession: Property, Authority, and Access to Natural Resources* (Malden: Wiley-Blackwell, 2010), pp. 1–22; Christian Lund, 'Property and Citizenship:

Conceptually Connecting Land Rights and Belonging in Africa',
Africa Spectrum 46(3) (2011): 71–5.

4 'land, n.1'. OED Online, June 2012, Oxford University Press,
www.oed.com (accessed 24 July 2012).

5 Michael Klare, *Rising Powers, Shrinking Planet: The New Geopolitics
of Energy* (New York: Metropolitan Books, 2008), p. 18; Jennifer
Clapp, *Food* (Cambridge: Polity, 2012), p. 98.

6 Benedict Anderson, *Imagined Communities: Reflections on the
Origin and Spread of Nationalism*, rev. edn (London and New York:
Verso, 1991).

7 Thongchai Winichakul, *Siam Mapped: A History of the Geo-Body of
a Nation* (Honolulu: University of Hawai'i Press, 1994).

8 Peter Vandergeest and Nancy Peluso, 'Territorialization and State
Power in Thailand', *Theory and Society* 24 (1995): 385–426.

9 Peter Schrag, *Paradise Lost: California's Experience, America's
Future*, updated edn (Berkeley and Los Angeles: University of
California Press, 2004), p. 141.

10 On the latter point, see Peter Vandergeest and Anusorn Unno, 'A
New Extraterritoriality? Aquaculture Certification, Sovereignty,
and Empire', *Political Geography* 31(6) (2012): 358–67.

11 See Edella Schlager and Elinor Ostrom, 'Property-Rights Regimes
and Natural Resources: A Conceptual Analysis', *Land Economics*
68(3) (1992): 250–1.

12 John F. Richards, 'Toward a Global System of Property Rights
in Land', in John F. Richards (ed.), *Land, Property, and the
Environment* (Oakland, CA: ICS Press, 2002), pp. 13–37.

CHAPTER 2 INTERSTATE STRUGGLES

1 For more on the concepts in this and the next paragraph, see
A. Claire Cutler, 'The Globalization of International Law,
Indigenous Identity, and the New Constitutionalism', in William
D. Coleman (ed.), *Property, Territory, Globalization: Struggles
over Autonomy* (Vancouver: University of British Columbia
Press, 2011), pp. 29–55; on the COW database, see Correlates of
War Project, 'State System Membership List, v2008.1', http://
correlatesofwar.org (accessed 26 July 2011).

2 This paragraph is based on Michael Biggs, 'Putting the State on
the Map: Cartography, Territory, and European State Formation',

Comparative Studies in Society and History 41(2) (1999): 375–405; Jordan Branch, 'Mapping the Sovereign State: Technology, Authority, and Systemic Change', *International Organization* 65(1) (2011): 1–36.

3 For the legal quotation, see Marc Zacher, 'The Territorial Integrity Norm: International Boundaries and the Use of Force', *International Organization* 55(2) (2001): 217; Charles Tilly, *Coercion, Capital and European States: AD 990–1992* (Cambridge, MA: Wiley-Blackwell, 1992), pp. 45–7.

4 Thongchai Winichakul, *Siam Mapped: A History of the Geo-Body of a Nation* (Honolulu: University of Hawai'i Press, 1994), ch. 3.

5 Marc Zacher, 'The Territorial Integrity Norm', p. 245; Stephen G. Brooks, 'The Globalization of Production Networks and the Changing Benefits of Conquest', *Journal of Conflict Resolution* 43(5) (1999): 653.

6 Robert Gilpin, *War and Change in World Politics* (Cambridge: Cambridge University Press, 1981), p. 23.

7 Human Security Centre, *Human Security Report 2005* (Vancouver: Human Security Centre, 2005), pp. 148, 18.

8 See David B. Carter and H. E. Goemans, 'The Making of the Territorial Order: New Borders and the Emergence of Interstate Conflict', *International Organization* 65(2) (2011): 275–309.

9 See Stephen G. Brooks, 'The Globalization of Production Networks'; Brooks, *Producing Security: Multinational Corporations, Globalization, and the Changing Calculus of Conflict* (Princeton and Oxford: Princeton University Press, 2005).

10 John Gallagher and Ronald Robinson, 'The Imperialism of Free Trade', *The Economic History Review* 6(1) (1953): 1–15.

11 Ron E. Hassner, 'The Path to Intractability: Time and the Entrenchment of Territorial Disputes', *International Security* 31(3) (2006/7): 107–38.

12 www.cia.gov/library/publications/the-world-factbook/ fields/2070.html (accessed 27 July 2012).

13 M. Taylor Fravel, 'Regime Insecurity and International Cooperation: Explaining China's Compromises in Territorial Disputes', *International Security* 30(2) (2005): 46–83.

14 Ron E. Hassner, 'The Path to Intractability', p. 107.

15 Carlos Ramos-Mrosovsky, 'International Law's Unhelpful Role in the Senkaku Islands', *University of Pennsylvania Journal of International Law* 29(4) (2008): 903–46.

16 For the information in this paragraph, see Alan M. Wachman, *Why Taiwan? Geostrategic Rationales for China's Territorial Integrity* (Stanford: Stanford University Press, 2007), p. 6; Shelley Rigger, *Taiwan Matters: Small Island, Global Powerhouse* (Lanham, MD: Rowman & Littlefield, 2011), chs 1 and 7; 'Helping Tibet would help Taiwan', *Taipei Times*, 31 January 2012.

17 Carole Blackburn, 'Differentiating Indigenous Citizenship: Seeking Multiplicity in Rights, Identity, and Sovereignty', *American Ethnologist* 36(1) (2009): 70. See also Patrick Macklem, *Indigenous Difference and the Constitution of Canada* (Toronto: University of Toronto Press, 2001).

CHAPTER 3 FRONTIERS

1 Figures estimated from graphs in Rodolphe De Koninck, 'Southeast Asian Agricultural Expansion in Global Perspective', in Rodolphe De Koninck, Stéphane Bernard and Jean-François Bissonnette (eds), *Borneo Transformed: Agricultural Expansion on the Southeast Asian Frontier* (Singapore: NUS Press, 2011), pp. 1–9.

2 Rodolphe De Koninck, 'The Peasantry as the Territorial Spearhead of the State in Southeast Asia: The Case of Vietnam', *Sojourn (Social Issues in Southeast Asia)* 11(2) (1996): 231–58.

3 This section draws mainly on Nasreen Ghufran, 'Pushtun Ethnonationalism and the Taliban Insurgency in the North West Frontier Province of Pakistan', *Asian Survey* 49(6) (2009): 1092–1114; Ahmed Rashid, *Descent into Chaos: The United States and the Failure of Nation Building in Pakistan, Afghanistan, and Central Asia* (New York: Viking, 2009); International Crisis Group, 'Pakistan's Tribal Areas: Appeasing the Militants', Asia Report No. 125, 11 December 2006, www.crisisgroup.org/en/regions/asia/south-asia/pakistan/125-pakistans-tribal-areas-appeasing-the-militants.aspx (accessed 1 August 2012); 'Pakistan: Countering Militancy in FATA', Asia Report No. 178, 21 October 2009, www.crisisgroup.org/en/regions/asia/south-asia/pakistan/178-pakistan-countering-militancy-in-fata.aspx (accessed 1 August 2012); Joshua T. White, 'The Shape of Frontier Rule: Governance and Transition, from the Raj to the Modern Pakistani Frontier', *Asian Security* 4(3) (2008): 219–43; Adnan Naseemullah, 'Violent Shades of Sovereignty: Variable State-Building and Insurgency

in South Asia', paper presented to the Annual Meetings of the American Political Science Association, Seattle, WA, 1–4 September 2011; Shuja Nawaz, *FATA – A Most Dangerous Place: Meeting the Challenge of Militancy and Terror in the Federally Administered Tribal Areas of Pakistan* (Washington, DC: Center for Strategic and International Studies, 2009).

4 A. Haroon Akram-Lodhi, 'Attacking the Pakhtuns', 29 October 2001, www.theglobalsite.ac.uk/justpeace/110akram.htm (accessed 23 January 2012).

5 Ainslie T. Embree, 'Frontiers into Boundaries: From the Traditional to the Modern State', in Richard G. Fox (ed.), *Realm and Region in Traditional India* (Durham, NC: Duke University Program in Comparative Studies on Southern Asia, 1977), p. 277.

6 International Crisis Group, 'Pakistan's Tribal Areas', pp. 6–7.

7 On the 'neo-Taliban', see Joshua T. White, 'The Shape of Frontier Rule', pp. 230 and 241 n. 42; on displaced people, International Crisis Group, 'Pakistan: Countering Militancy', p. 8.

8 Ahmed Rashid, *Descent into Chaos*, p. 275; International Crisis Group, 'Pakistan's Tribal Areas', pp. 5–9, and 'Pakistan: Countering Militancy', p. 11; Joshua T. White, 'The Shape of Frontier Rule', pp. 236–7.

9 Matthew Green, 'US hopes tribal highway will be path to stability', *Financial Times*, 11 February 2011.

10 Particularly helpful sources for this section have been Sarah Bonesteel (ed.), *Canada's Relationship with the Inuit: A History of Policy and Program Development* (Indian and Northern Affairs Canada, 2006); Natalia Loukacheva, 'Nunavut and Canadian Arctic Sovereignty', *Journal of Canadian Studies* 43(2) (2009): 82–108; Mary Simon, 'Inuit and the Canadian Arctic: Sovereignty Begins at Home', *Journal of Canadian Studies* 43(2) (2009): 250–60; Frances Abele and Thierry Rodon, 'Inuit Diplomacy in the Global Era: The Strengths of Multilateral Internationalism', *Canadian Foreign Policy* 13(3) (2007): 45–63; Shelagh Grant, *Polar Imperative: A History of Arctic Sovereignty in North America* (Vancouver: Douglas & McIntyre, 2010).

11 Frances Abele and Thierry Rodon, 'Inuit Diplomacy', p. 50.

12 Sarah Bonesteel, *Canada's Relationship with the Inuit*, pp. 37–9.

13 Quoted in Whitney Lackenbauer, 'The Canadian Rangers: A "Postmodern" Militia that Works', *Canadian Military Journal* 6(4) (2005–6): 49–60.

14 Harper quotations from Mary Simon, 'Inuit and the Canadian
    Arctic', p. 252, and Natalia Loukacheva, 'Nunavut and Canadian
    Arctic Sovereignty', p. 84; Charest quoted in Bernard Simon,
    'Canada Boosts Claim to Northwest Passage', *Financial Times*, 11
    May 2011.
15 Mary Simon, 'Inuit and the Canadian Arctic', pp. 251–2; Natalia
    Loukacheva, 'Nunavut and Canadian Arctic Sovereignty',
    p. 99.
16 Zellen quoted in Shelagh Grant, *Polar Imperative*, p. 460;
    Whitney Lackenbauer, 'The Canadian Rangers'.

CHAPTER 4 LAND BOOMS

1 For a positive take on agribusiness in the *cerrado*, see 'The miracle
   of the cerrado', *The Economist*, 26 August 2010; for a more critical
   one, Fred Pearce, *The Land Grabbers: The New Fight over Who
   Owns the Earth* (Boston: Beacon Press, 2012), ch. 10.
2 Data in this and the following paragraphs are from UNCTAD,
   *World Investment Report 2011: Non-Equity Modes of International
   Production and Development* (New York and Geneva: United
   Nations, 2011). The quotation in the next paragraph is from p. xi.
3 Karl Polanyi, *The Great Transformation: The Political and Economic
   Origins of Our Time* (Boston: Beacon Press, 1957).
4 Michael Levien, 'The Land Question: Special Economic Zones
   and the Political Economy of Dispossession in India', *Journal of
   Peasant Studies* 39(3–4) (2012): 944; see also 'Special Economic
   Zones and Accumulation by Dispossession in India', *Journal of
   Agrarian Change* 11(4) (2011): 454–83.
5 On the US programmes, see Sam Raphael and Doug Stokes,
   'Globalizing West African Oil: US "Energy Security" and the
   Global Economy', *International Affairs* 87(4) (2011): 918; on the
   World Bank Group, see The Oakland Institute, 'Understanding
   Land Investment Deals in Africa: The Role of the World Bank
   Group', Land Deal Brief, December 2011.
6 For AgroGlobe, see Fred Pearce, *The Land Grabbers*, p. 33; for
   the other projects, see the February 2012 GRAIN land grab deal
   dataset at www.grain.org/article/entries/4479-grain-releases-data-
   set-with-over-400-global-land-grabs.pdf (accessed 11 May 2012).
7 These estimates from the World Bank, the Global Land Project,

the Land Deal Politics Initiative and Oxfam respectively are cited in Fred Pearce, *The Land Grabbers*, pp. viii–ix.

8 Derek Headey and Shenggen Fan, 'Anatomy of a Crisis: The Causes and Consequences of Surging Food Prices', *Agricultural Economics* 39 (Supplement) (2008): 376.

9 Klaus Deininger, 'Challenges Posed by the New Wave of Farmland Investment', *Journal of Peasant Studies* 38(2) (2011): 236; www.responsibleagroinvestment.org/rai/node/256 (accessed 18 October 2011).

10 Saturnino M. Borras Jr and Jennifer Franco, 'Political Dynamics of Land-grabbing in Southeast Asia: Understanding Europe's Role' (Amsterdam: Transnational Institute, 2011).

11 The World Bank, *Rising Global Interest in Farmland: Can it Yield Sustainable and Equitable Benefits?* (Washington, DC: The World Bank, 2010), pp. xiv, 35–6.

12 Liz Alden Wily, 'The Tragedy of Public Lands: The Fate of the Commons under Global Commercial Pressure' (CIRAD and International Land Coalition, 2011).

13 Shepard Daniel with Anuradha Mittal, '(Mis)Investment in Agriculture: The Role of the International Finance Corporation in Global Land Grabs' (Oakland, CA: The Oakland Institute, 2010), p. 24.

14 Laura A. German, George Schoneveld and Esther Mwangi, 'Processes of Large-Scale Land Acquisition by Investors: Case Studies from Sub-Saharan Africa', paper presented to the International Conference on Global Land Grabbing (Institute of Development Studies, University of Sussex, 6–8 April 2011); The World Bank, *Rising Global Interest in Farmland*, p. xiv.

15 Indian economic statistics calculated by the author from World Bank data downloaded on 30 October 2011. On Indian SEZs, see Michael Levien, 'Special Economic Zones' and 'The Land Question'.

16 Michael Levien, 'The Land Question', p. 946.

17 Michael Levien, 'Special Economic Zones', p. 459.

18 Michael Levien, 'Special Economic Zones', p. 464.

19 Michael Levien, 'Special Economic Zones', p. 477.

20 Michael Goldman, 'Speculative Urbanism and the Making of the Next World City', *International Journal of Urban and Regional Research* 35(3) (2011): 555–81. The quotation in this paragraph is from p. 567, those in the next are from pp. 556 and 574, and the final quotation is from p. 557.

CHAPTER 5 TITLING AND CONSERVATION

1 The conceptual framework of this chapter draws substantially on Derek Hall, Philip Hirsch and Tania Murray Li, *Powers of Exclusion: Land Dilemmas in Southeast Asia* (Singapore and Honolulu: NUS Press and University of Hawai'i Press, 2011), chs 2 and 3.

2 The World Bank, *Land Policies for Growth and Poverty Reduction* (Oxford: The World Bank and Oxford University Press, 2003), p. 24.

3 Hernando de Soto, *The Mystery of Capital: Why Capitalism Triumphs in the West and Fails Everywhere Else* (New York: Basic Books, 2000).

4 http://ild.org.pe/eu/our-work/ (accessed 20 September 2011).

5 Commission on Legal Empowerment of the Poor, *Making the Law Work for Everyone: Volume 1* (New York: Commission on Legal Empowerment of the Poor and United Nations Development Programme, 2008); The World Bank, *Land Policies*.

6 V. Rattanabirabongse et al., 'The Thailand Land Titling Project – Thirteen Years of Experience', *Land Use Policy* 15(1) (1998): 11; Lynn Holstein, 'Towards Best Practice from World Bank Experience in Land Titling and Registration', October 1996, available at http://sfrc.ifas.ufl.edu/geomatics/publications/land_conf96/HolsteinPD.PDF (accessed 20 September 2012).

7 Kees Jansen and Esther Roquas, 'Modernizing Insecurity: The Land Titling Project in Honduras', *Development and Change* 18(1) (1998): 102.

8 See, for instance, Kees Jansen and Esther Roquas, 'Modernizing Insecurity'; Rattanabirabongse et al., 'The Thailand Land Titling Project', pp. 3–23 ; Rikke B. Broegaard, 'Land Access and Titling in Nicaragua', *Development and Change* 40(1) (2009): 149–69; Megan Ybarra, 'Violent Visions of an Ownership Society: The Land Administration Project in Petén, Guatemala', *Land Use Policy* 26(1) (2009): 44–54; Robin Biddulph, 'Tenure Security Interventions in Cambodia: Testing Bebbington's Approach to Development Geography', *Geografiska Annaler: Series B, Human Geography* 93(3) (2011): 223–36.

9 Tor A. Benjaminsen, Stein Holden, Christian Lund and Espen Sjaastad, 'Formalisation of Land Rights: Some Empirical

Evidence from Mali, Niger and South Africa', *Land Use Policy* 28(1) (2009): 31.

10 Kees Jansen and Esther Roquas, 'Modernizing Insecurity', pp. 97–9.

11 The IUCN describes itself as 'the world's oldest and largest global environmental network', and has more than 1,000 governmental and NGO member organizations. www.iucn.org/ (accessed 27 September 2011).

12 For Figure 5.1, see IUCN and UNEP-WCMC, *The World Database on Protected Areas* (WDPA) (Cambridge: UNEP-WCMC, February 2012). For Table 5.1, see www.wdpa.org/Statistics.aspx, (accessed 9 October 2011). Note that the methods of calculating protected area in Figure 5.1 and Table 5.1 differ. I am grateful to UNEP and WCMC for permission to use this data.

13 The Ramsar Convention and its mission: www.ramsar.org/cda/en/ramsar-about-mission/main/ramsar/1-36-53_4000_0__ (accessed 27 September 2011).

14 'Science, Sentiment, and Advocacy: An Interview with Richard Leakey', *Yellowstone Science* 10(3) (2002): 11.

15 Dan Brockington, Rosaleen Duffy and Jim Igoe, *Nature Unbound: Conservation, Capitalism and the Future of Protected Areas* (London and Sterling, VA: Earthscan, 2008), p. 150.

16 Tania Murray Li, 'Practices of Assemblage and Community Forest Management', *Economy and Society* 36(2) (2007): 269.

17 Paige West, *Conservation is Our Government Now: The Politics of Ecology in Papua New Guinea* (Durham, NC and London: Duke University Press, 2007). The quotations in this paragraph are from pp. 117–18 and 5, and that in the next is from p. 39, those in the last paragraph of this section are from pp. 35 and 227.

CHAPTER 6 SOCIAL MOVEMENTS

1 See p. 53 of the report, available at www.un.org/esa/socdev/unpfii/documents/SOWIP_web.pdf (accessed 30 July 2012).

2 See http://pwccc.wordpress.com/2010/04/30/final-conclusions-working-group-nff17-indigenous-peoples/#more-1644 (accessed 1 August 2012).

3 Margaret Keck and Kathryn Sikkink, *Activists Beyond Borders* (Ithaca, NY: Cornell University Press, 1998).

4 For this paragraph, see M. J. Peterson, 'How the Indigenous got Seats at the UN Table', *Review of International Organization* 5(2) (2010): 197–225; Roderic Pitty and Shannara Smith, 'The Indigenous Challenge to Westphalian Sovereignty', *Australian Journal of Political Science* 46(1) (2011): 121–39.

5 Pitty and Smith, 'The Indigenous Challenge', p. 126.

6 Gaetano Pentassuglia, 'Towards a Jurisprudential Articulation of Indigenous Land Rights', *The European Journal of International Law* 22(1) (2011): 165–202; Rachel Sieder, '"Emancipation" or "Regulation"? Law, Globalization and Indigenous Peoples' Rights in Post-War Guatemala', *Economy and Society* 40(2) (2011): 239–65.

7 For this paragraph, see Saturnino M. Borras Jr, 'La Vía Campesina and its Global Campaign for Agrarian Reform', in Saturnino M. Borras Jr, Marc Edelman and Cristóbal Kay (eds), *Transnational Agrarian Movements Confronting Globalization* (Malden, MA: Wiley-Blackwell, 2008, pp. 91–121); Borras, 'The Politics of Transnational Agrarian Movements', *Development and Change* 41(5) (2010): 771–803; Marc Edelman and Carwil James, 'Peasants' Rights and the UN System: Quixotic Struggle? Or Emancipatory Idea Whose Time has Come?' *Journal of Peasant Studies* 38(1) (2011): 81–108.

8 For this paragraph and the next, see Saturnino M. Borras Jr, 'La Vía Campesina'.

9 'Declaration of Rights of Peasants – Women and Men', document adopted by the Vía Campesina International Coordinating Committee in Seoul, March 2009, available at http://viacampesina.net/downloads/PDF/EN-3.pdf (accessed 27 November 2011).

10 Marc Edelman and Carwil James, 'Peasants' Rights and the UN System', quotation from p. 95.

11 Statistics on Chinese GDP growth, per capita GDP and urban population downloaded from databank.worldbank.org on 22 November 2011. The following paragraphs are based primarily on You-Tien Hsing, *The Great Urban Transformation: Politics of Land and Property in China* (Oxford and New York: Oxford University Press, 2010); Kevin J. O'Brien and Lianjiang Li, *Rightful Resistance in Rural China* (Cambridge: Cambridge University Press, 2006); Kathy Le Mons Walker, 'From Covert to Overt: Everyday Peasant Politics in China and the Implications for Transnational Agrarian

Movements', *Journal of Agrarian Change* 8(2 & 3) (2008): 462–88. See also Chen Guidi and Chuntao Wu, *Will the Boat Sink the Water? The Life of China's Peasants* (New York: PublicAffairs, 2006).

12 On the issues discussed in this paragraph, see You-Tien Hsing, *The Great Urban Transformation*, pp. 5–7, 94–8.

13 Kathy Le Mons Walker, 'From Covert to Overt', p. 475; You-Tien Hsing, *The Great Urban Transformation*, p. 213.

14 Kathy Le Mons Walker, 'From Covert to Overt', p. 467.

15 Kevin O'Brien and Lianjiang Li, *Rightful Resistance in Rural China*, p. 34.

16 You-Tien Hsing, *The Great Urban Transformation*, p. 124.

17 Kevin O'Brien and Lianjiang Li, *Rightful Resistance in Rural China*, p. 28.

18 You-Tien Hsing, *The Great Urban Transformation*, p. 203.

19 Marc Edelman, 'Transnational Organizing in Agrarian Central America: Histories, Challenges, Prospects', in Saturnino M. Borras Jr, Marc Edelman and Cristóbal Kay (eds), *Transnational Agrarian Movements Confronting Globalization* (Malden, MA: Wiley-Blackwell, 2008), p. 83.

CHAPTER 7 CONCLUSION

1 My sources for the following paragraphs are Michael Eilenberg, *At the Edges of States: Dynamics of State Formation in the Indonesian Borderlands* (Leiden: KILTV Press, 2011); and Lesley Potter, 'Resource Periphery, Corridor, Heartland: Contesting Land Use in the Kalimantan/Malaysia Borderlands', *Asia Pacific Viewpoint* 50(1) (2009): 88–106.

2 Michael Eilenberg, *At the Edges of States*, p. 236.

3 www.laphroaig.com/plot. My plot is number 518722.

Index